ASIA PACIFIC ECONOMIC COOPERATION (APEC): CURRENT ISSUES AND BACKGROUND

Asia Pacific Economic Cooperation (APEC): Current Issues and Background

Sandra L. Downing
Editor

Nova Science Publishers, Inc.
New York

Senior Editors: Susan Boriotti and Donna Dennis
Coordinating Editor: Tatiana Shohov
Office Manager: Annette Hellinger
Graphics: Wanda Serrano and Matt Dallow
Editorial Production: Maya Columbus, Alexis Klestov, Vladimir Klestov, Matthew Kozlowski and Lorna Loperfido
Circulation: Ave Maria Gonzalez, Vera Popovic, Sean Corkery, Raymond Davis, Melissa Diaz, Magdalena Nuñez, Marlene Nuñez and Jeannie Pappas
Communications and Acquisitions: Serge P. Shohov
Marketing: Cathy DeGregory

Library of Congress Cataloging-in-Publication Data
Available Upon Request

ISBN: 1-59033-698-4.

400 Oser Ave, Suite 1600
Hauppauge, New York 11788-3619
Tele. 631-231-7269 Fax 631-231-8175
e-mail: Novascience@earthlink.net
Web Site: http://www.novapublishers.com

Printed in the United States of America

CONTENTS

PREFACE

In 1989, President George Bush was President of the United States the Asia-Pacific Economic Cooperation (APEC) forum was established to promote economic integration around the Pacific Rim and to sustain economic growth. APEC currently has 21 members: Australia; Brunei Darussalam; Canada; Chile; Hong Kong, China; Indonesia; Japan; Republic of Korea; Malaysia; Mexico; New Zealand; Papua New Guinea; Peru; Republic of the Philippines; Russia; Singapore; Chinese Taipei; Thailand; USA; Vietnam. The United States, recognizing the value of top-level meetings to advance the work of creating a Pacific community, invited member economies' leaders to Blake Island, Washington, to meet informally to discuss major issues in the APEC region. This gathering of economic leaders has become the single most important institution in the Asia Pacific region. It brings top level attention to APEC's vision of free trade and investment as well as providing a forum for leaders to meet on a regular basis both as a group and bilaterally to discuss current issues and resolve disputes.

The Asia Pacific Economic Cooperation (APEC) forum is an organization of eighteen economies surrounding the Pacific Ocean that promotes open trade and closer economic cooperation in the Asia/Pacific region. Its membership includes the United States, Canada, Mexico, and Chile in the Americas, Japan, South Korea, China, Taiwan, and Hong Kong in East Asia, the ASEAN nations of Indonesia, Brunei, Malaysia, Singapore, Thailand, and The Philippines, plus the Oceanic nations of Australia, New Zealand, and Papua New Guinea.

The economic health of the APEC region is vitally important to America's continued prosperity. Economic growth across the APEC region waned this year, largely in response to the slowing US economy and the weakening global demand for many of the Asian members' exports (particularly electronics). Many members have lowered their 2001 growth projections in light of poor performance during the first half of the year, although most will still post positive results.

APEC is of interest to the Congress because it is committed to dismantling all barriers to trade and investment among its members by the year 2010 for industrialized member economies or 2020 for the remainder. This future free-trade area would cover nearly half the world's population, 60 percent of the world's gross domestic product, and 40 percent of world trade. APEC may define the framework for America's future trading relationships with the fast-growing Asian region. If APEC achieves its goals, the United States would establish free trade with nations, such as Japan and China, that are responsible for about half of the U.S, trade deficit and which account for many of the U.S. trade problems. Since trade barriers in Asia are higher than those in the United States, however, the United States seems to have more to gain in the process than it loses. Free trade among Asian nations, moreover, may allow more Asian exports to be absorbed at home rather than being directed at the U.S. market.

On November 19, 1995, the leaders of APEC met in Osaka, Japan, where they agreed to an Action Agenda that is intended to translate the vision of an APEC free-trade area into reality. This Action Agenda is the template for future APEC work to accomplish the three common goals of (1) trade and investment liberalization, (2) trade and investment facilitation, and (3) economic and technical cooperation. The Agenda laid out nine general principles which are to guide individual APEC members in devising national Action Plans (to be submitted in 1996) to attain the goal. The Action Plans are to be implemented starting in January 1997. A question is whether, and at what point in the APEC process, fast-track authority would be necessary.

There was considerable disagreement among APEC members over whether the principle of comprehensiveness in removing barriers to trade would apply to all products and commodities. Japan, China, South Korea, and Taiwan succeeded in inserting a principle of flexibility which arguably means that members would have some flexibility in liberalizing trade in sensitive sectors, such as agriculture. China also tried to obtain a definition of non-discrimination that would assure it of most-favored-nation treatment by the United States.

In terms of political feasibility, a key question remains to be answered. Would the public support a free trade area encompassing all major Asian and Pacific economies? How would the American people respond to a free-trade area that included China, Japan, and South Korea? Import-sensitive industries, such as textiles and apparel, also would likely oppose free imports from Asia.

This compelling book about APEC and its background, goals and problems, provides the reader with the necessary information on the crucial role that it plays.

A revived Asia-Pacific region means more exports from and investments by U.S. companies, more jobs for Americans and more U.S. economic growth.

Chapter 1

ASIA PACIFIC ECONOMIC COOPERATION: OVERVIEW AND BACKGROUND*

Tatiana Shohov (Editor)

Asia-Pacific Economic Cooperation (APEC) was established in 1989 in response to the growing interdependence among Asia-Pacific economies. It is is the premier forum for facilitating economic growth, cooperation, trade and investment in the Asia-Pacific region. From its modest beginning as an informal Ministerial-level dialogue group with 12 members, APEC has become a formidable regional forum, especially with the introduction of the annual informal Economic Leaders' Meeting in 1993. Its goal is *to advance economic dynamism and sense of community within the Asia-Pacific region*. Today there are 21 member economies comprising some 2.5 billion people, a combined gross domestic product of over US$19 trillion accounting for 47 percent of world trade. APEC has established itself as the primary regional vehicle for promoting open trade and practical economic and technical cooperation. APEC is the premier forum for facilitating economic growth, cooperation, trade and investment in the Asia-Pacific region. As the primary regional vehicle for promoting trade and investment and practical economic cooperation, the end result of APEC's activities includes increased employment opportunities and community development.

* Excerpted from: http://usinfo.state.gov/regional/ea/apec/mexico/fsapecoverview.html

APEC is working to achieve what are referred to as the 'Bogor Goals' of free and open trade and investment in the Asia-Pacific by 2010 for developed economies and 2020 for developing economies. APEC has identified three specific areas that are crucial to achieving the Bogor Goals. These three pillars are:

- Trade and Investment Liberalisaton
- Business Facilitation, and
- Economic and Technical Cooperation.

Since its inception in 1989, APEC has helped to reduce tariffs and other barriers to trade in the Asia-Pacific region. APEC has also worked to ensure the safe and efficient movement of goods, services and people across the borders in the region through facilitating practical policy formulation in APEC economies and by facilitating economic and technical cooperation.

Asia Pacific Economic Cooperation (APEC)

The Beginning

The APEC forum was established in 1989 to promote economic cooperation and integration in the Pacific region. The United States was a driving force in APEC's creation, as a means of anchoring the United States more firmly in the region in the post-Cold War era. APEC has grown to 21 members, including four other economies in the western hemisphere (Canada, Chile, Mexico and Peru). The first APEC Leaders Meeting occurred in 1993 when the United States invited member economies' leaders to Blake Island, Washington. In 1995, APEC established a business advisory body, called the APEC Business Advisory Council (ABAC), which consists of three business executives from each member economy.

The Bogor Goals

At Blake Island, Leaders called for continued reduction of trade and investment barriers, envisioning an "Asia-Pacific community" that promotes prosperity through cooperation. In 1994, Leaders at Bogor, Indonesia, set the goals of reaching free trade and investment by 2010 for developed economies, and 2020 for developing economies.

Strengthening Multilateral and Regional Trade

APEC's early successes included helping to build consensus for conclusion of the Uruguay Round in 1994 and its role in pioneering the 1996 Information Technology Agreement. In Shanghai, APEC's strong push for a new Trade Round and support for a robust program of trade capacity-building assistance was critical to the successful launch of the Doha Development Agenda a few weeks later.

APEC has taken a number of steps to liberalize regional trade. For example, in 1999 it launched the APEC Open Skies Agreement, the first multilateral air services liberalization agreement in the world. In 2001, Leaders endorsed the U.S.-proposed "Shanghai Accord" which emphasizes implementation of APEC's commitments to open markets, structural reform, and capacity building. As part of the Accord, Leaders committed to develop and implement APEC transparency standards, reduce trade transaction costs in the Asia-Pacific region by 5 percent over 5 years, and pursue trade liberalization policies relating to information technology goods and services.

Counterterrorism

Following the September 11, 2001, terrorist attacks, Leaders in Shanghai pledged counterterrorism cooperation. In Los Cabos this year, Leaders will build on the Shanghai Statement through commitments designed to protect key Pacific Rim infrastructure -- trade, finance and information systems -- from terrorist exploitation and attack.

APEC Organization

APEC operates by consensus. In 1991, members committed themselves to conducting their activities and work programs on the basis of open dialogue with equal respect for the views of all participants.

Ministerial and Senior Officials Meetings

The APEC Chair, which rotates annually among members, is responsible for hosting the annual ministerial meeting of foreign and economic ministers.

At the 1989 Canberra Ministerial Meeting, it was agreed that it would be appropriate that every alternate ministerial meeting be held in an ASEAN economy. Senior Officials Meetings (SOM) are held regularly prior to every ministerial meeting. APEC senior officials make recommendations to the Ministers and carry out their decisions. They oversee and coordinate, with approval from Ministers, the budgets and work programs of the APEC fora. APEC member economies have hosted a number of other ministerial meetings for Ministers of education, energy, environment and sustainable development, finance, human resources development, regional science and technology cooperation, small and medium enterprises, telecommunications and information industry, trade, and transportation.

APEC operates by consensus. In 1991, members committed themselves to conducting their activities and work programs on the basis of open dialogue with equal respect for the views of all participants.

APEC Business Advisory Council

In 1995 APEC Economic Leaders established a permanent council composed of up to three senior business people from each member economy to provide advice on the implementation of APEC action plans and on other specific business/private sector priorities. Chairmanship of ABAC rotates each year according to which economy chairs APEC. The 2002 ABAC Chair is Mr Javier Prieto, Senior Vice President for External Affairs for CEMEX of Mexico.

ABAC has presented six published reports to APEC Leaders on the theme of "APEC Means Business," containing specific recommendations for improving regional business conditions and expanding trade and investment. ABAC's 2001 report focused on proposals to help APEC member economies stay on track with trade and investment liberalization and facilitation, build stronger financial systems, and improve access to new opportunities through technological progress. Specific ABAC recommendations targeted the need for accelerated banking and market capital reforms; intensified capacity-building in the financial system; encouraging Leaders to renounce the use of food embargoes; aligning standards and conformance to international standards; adopting policies to enhance the use of e-learning, and to adopt policies that are "small business- friendly." ABAC members have the opportunity to discuss their recommendations at their annual dialogue with APEC Leaders in Los Cabos, Mexico in October and at various ministerial meetings throughout the year.

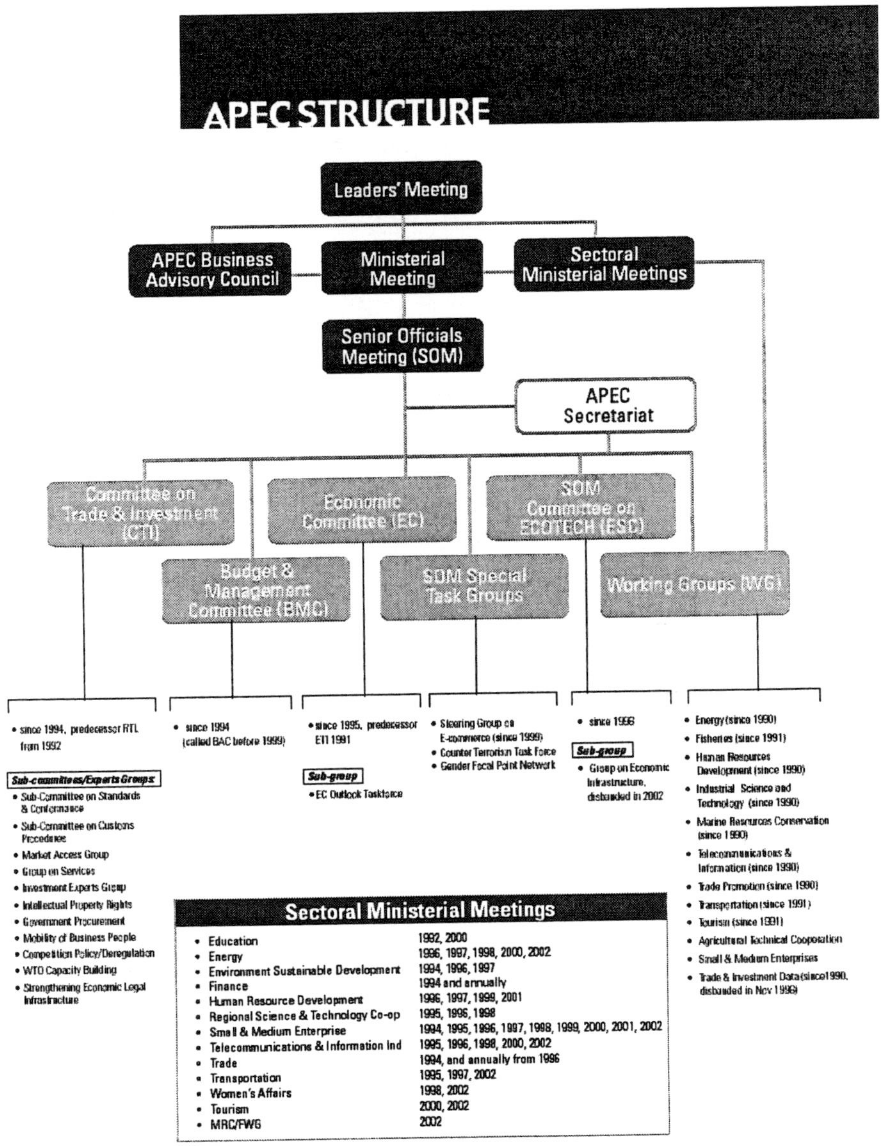

APEC Organizational Chart

APEC Fora

At each year's Ministerial Meeting, members define and fund work programs for APEC's three committees, eleven working groups and other APEC fora.

QUESTION & ANSWER

Q: What does "APEC" stand for?

A: "APEC" stands for "Asia-Pacific Economic Cooperation".

Q: When and why "APEC" was established?

A: "APEC" was established in 1989 in response to the growing interdependence among Asia-Pacific economies. Its goal is to advance Asia-Pacific economic dynamism and sense of community.

Q: Who are the members of "APEC" and when did they join the "APEC"?

A: When APEC was established in 1989, there were 12 founding members, namely Australia, Brunei Darussalam, Canada, Indonesia, Japan, Republic of Korea, Malaysia, New Zealand, Republic of the Philippines, Singapore, Thailand and Unites States. In November 1991, APEC accepted three new members, namely People's Republic of China, Hong Kong (its designation has been changed to Hong Kong, China since 1 July 1997) and Chinese Taipei. In November 1993, APEC accepted Mexico and Papua New Guinea as new members. At the same time, APEC decided that Chile would become a full member in November 1994. In November 1997, APEC Economic Leaders welcomed Peru, Russia and Vietnam as new members of the APEC community effective in 1998. Their formal membership started in November 1998.

Q: Who are the "Observers" of APEC?

A: There are three observers, namely Association of Southeast Asian Nations (ASEAN) Secretariat, Pacific Economic Cooperation Council (PECC) and Pacific Islands Forum Secretariat (PIF).

Q: What does "Members-designate" mean?

A: "Members-designate" is the status of Peru, Russia and Vietnam in APEC during the period from January 1998 to November 1998. It is a transitional arrangement to give adequate lead time for these three economies to get acquainted with the APEC affairs. As members-designate, they were invited to attend all the meetings as observers during the transitional period.

Q: What does "EVSL" mean?

A: "EVSL" means "Early Voluntary Sectoral Liberalization". The concept was presented by the APEC Economic Leaders in 1996 to identify potential sectors where early voluntary liberalization would have a positive impact on trade, investment, and economic growth in the individual APEC economies as well as in the region.

Q: How many sectors are involved in the "EVSL" process?

A: Fifteen (15) sectors were identified in 1997. They are: environmental goods and services; fish and fish products; toys; forest products; gems and jewellery; medical equipment and instruments; chemicals; energy sector; telecommunications mutual recognition arrangement (MRA); food sector; natural and synthetic rubber; fertilizers; automotive; oilseeds and oilseed products and civil aircraft. The first nine (9) sectors belonged to fast track sectors.

Q: When and where was the Secretariat established?

A: In September 1992, the 4th APEC Ministerial Meeting agreed to set up a secretariat as a supporting mechanism and accepted the offer from Singapore to host the Secretariat. The Secretariat was officially established on 12 February, 1993 in Singapore.

Q: What is the composition of the Secretariat staff?

A: The Secretariat has two-category of staff. The first category is Professional Staff Members (PSMs) which are seconded from the government of member economies. The other is Supportive Staff Members (SSMs) which are openly recruited in Singapore.

Q: How can I participate in the APEC activities?

A: All the APEC activities are open to all APEC member economies. Non-member economies, regional/international organizations as well as others can participate, as guests, in some of the activities, subject to approval/agreement of APEC. For more details, please refer to **Non-Member Participation.**

Q: How is the APEC decision-making process?

A: APEC operates by consensus. Members conduct their activities and work programs on the basis of open dialogue with equal respect for the views of all participants.

Q: How does APEC select the Chair?

A: The APEC Chair rotates annually among APEC members. The APEC Chair is responsible for hosting the annual ministerial meeting of foreign and economic ministers.

Q: Where can I get the trade statistics of APEC member economies?

A: Please see the " Economic Indicators " table.

Q: Where can I get the meeting documents?

A: Please visit the "Virtual Library" in the APEC website. Normally, the meeting summary conclusions will be available after 30 days of the meeting.

Consolidated Guidelines On Non-Member Participation In APEC Working Group Activities

Introduction

It is understood that APEC Working Group (WG) activities are those activities approved by the APEC WGs and participated in by a large number of APEC members, including WG meetings, workshops, seminars, symposiums, training courses, etc..

In general, non-member economies, organisations and business/private sector representatives may apply and/or be invited to APEC WG activities subject to the following guidelines.

Categories of Participants

In general, APEC has only four categories of participants in its WG activities:

- *Members* (It is up to each member to decide whom to include in its own member delegation);
- *APEC Secretariat;*
- *Observers* [currently the Secretariat of the Association of South East Asian Nations (ASEAN Secretariat), the Pacific Economic Cooperation Council (PECC) and the Pacific Islands Forum Secretariat (PIF)]; and
- *Guests*, which include all participants other than the three categories above.

Within the category of "guests" there are three sub-categories:

- non-member economies;
- other relevant regional/international organisations and bodies; and
- business/private sector representatives not included as part of member economy delegations.

Principles

1. It is important that on the one hand APEC neither gives the appearance of being a closed shop nor cuts itself off from useful contact with non-members, while on the other that it gives due weight to the need for consolidation and effectiveness.

2. The following principles should be used in considering any application/proposed invitation:

    a. Non-member participation in any WG should be determined by the individual WG concerned by consensus, subject to approval by the SOM;
    b. Each application/proposed invitation should be considered on its own merits;
    c. While geographic location should be given primary weight, consideration should be given to specific expertise or information which the applicant/invitee possesses;
    d. The WG must be satisfied that the applicant/invitee can make a significant contribution to the work of the Group; and
    e. Participation in the WG must be clearly understood not to imply any tacit endorsement of future membership or observer status in other APEC activities.

3. This last principle is particularly important. There must be no linkage between participation in APEC WGs and any application for a full membership of APEC. In other words, participation in a WG is neither necessary nor sufficient for a successful application to become an APEC member.

Management (Procedures)

The participation by non-members should be managed as follows:

1. The APEC Secretariat in Singapore should act as the sole point of contact for non-members who wish to participate in APEC activities and for proposed invitations by APEC members;
2. Once consensus has been reached in the WG concerned, the Lead Shepherd should seek covering approval from the Senior Officials of all member economies through the APEC Secretariat;
3. Once the application/proposed invitation is approved, the terms of participation should then be conveyed to the guests in standard form by the APEC Secretariat;
4. Guest status should be granted for the calendar year in which the application/proposed invitation is made and for the following two calendar years, with renewal of participation subject to the same procedure as a new application/proposed invitation;
5. For detailed procedures on processing an application or proposed invitation, see Annex; and
6. Guest participation in one-off non-policy APEC activities such as symposia, workshops and seminars, including those organised by APEC forum other than WGs, and joint WG activities with other organisations can be approved by the relevant WG or forum by consensus on the delegated authority of the SOM. In such cases , the rules above do not apply.

Terms of Non-Member Participation

The following terms spell out the rights of participation by non-members in APEC Working Group meetings, and the supporting role of the Chair in controlling non-member participation in such meetings and ensuring that it conforms with all APEC procedures and requirements:

1. Guests may be invited/allowed by the Chair to address a WG meeting on an agreed topic where this is relevant to the item under consideration and while the views may be taken into account by the WG, the guests cannot take part the in decision-making process;

2. Guests may be invited by the Chair to respond to questions that arise in a WG meeting;
3. Guests, with the agreement of the Chair, may be permitted to circulate documents on relevant subjects during APEC WG meetings;
4. Guests should respect the confidentiality of the discussions of the meetings and the documents received;
5. Guests and observers should be invited to leave the meeting room when the agenda of non-member participation is discussed; and
6. The Chair may also convene *closed sessions of WG meetings* excluding observers and guests.

It is further recommended that when non-members will be taking part in WG meetings, the Chair convene preparatory discussions, excluding guests, to arrive at a consensus among members present as to possible topics which the non-member participants may be invited by the Chair to address during the open session, and the type of information or documentation to be made available to participating non-members.

PROCEDURES ON PROCESSING APPLICATIONS/PROPOSED INVITATIONS FOR NON-MEMBER PARTICIPATION

1. Applications/proposed invitations for all non-member participation in a WG should be forwarded to the APEC Secretariat for proper recording and transmission to the Lead Shepherd.
2. As soon as an application/proposed invitation is made in writing for non-member participation, the Lead Shepherd should immediately inform the Members of the WG, consulting their views.
3. When informing the WG Members, the Lead Shepherd might choose to offer views on whether or not the applicant/proposed invitee meets the principles adopted by APEC Ministers.
4. The Lead Shepherd should remind that the question posed *is a "technical" one*, i.e. to develop a view with regard to points 2c and 2d under the principles of the approved guidelines.
5. Replies may come in any form, including oral responses.
6. The Lead Shepherd should be left to ensure that consensus is sought on participation of non-members. The Lead Shepherd should determine, in consultation with the WG, whether silence constitutes consent or dissent.

The agreed modalities should be communicated by the Lead Shepherd to the SOM.

7. A thirty-day time limit for response by the WG to the Secretariat should be encouraged.
8. The Lead Shepherd must, as soon as possible after the deadline, report through the Secretariat the results of the consultation to the Chair of the SOM for circulation to Senior Officials. If additional information is required from the applicant/proposed invitee, the Secretariat will seek such information at the same time the report is forwarded to the Chair.
9. In making a final consideration on the application/proposed invitation, Senior Officials will bear in mind both the broader context and the "technical" consultation as per paragraph 4 above.
10. A positive decision taken on an application/proposed invitation will be valid for the calendar year in which the application/invitation is made and for the following two calendar years. To renew such non-member participation, the same procedures as a new application/proposed invitation will apply.
11. Prior to a decision, when approached by any inquiries about the status of the application/proposed invitation, the Secretariat, Lead Shepherd or any member economy should respond with a standard formulation, "When a decision is made we will inform you."
12. WGs may establish their own set of specifications to guide them in the technical evaluation of applications/proposed invitations. These criteria, however, will have to be consistent with the overall guidelines for non-member participation in WGs as approved by Ministers.
13. WGs should advance decisions on non-member participation on an inter-sessional basis and SOM approval can also be attained on this basis.
14. When Senior Officials have reached a decision, the Secretariat will forward the decision to the non-member making application/being invited to participate. With reference to a positive decision, the Secretariat will forward a copy of the "Terms of Non-Member Participation" as well as the name and address of the Lead Shepherd who will be copied on all correspondence.

Economic Indicators

Member Economy and Year Joined	Area ('000 sq km)	Population (million)	Current Price GDP (US$bn)	Current GDP per capita (US$)	Exports, fob (US$bn)	Imports, cif (US$bn)
Australia (1989)	7,682	19.1	380	18,421	64	67
Brunei Darussalam (1989)	6	0.3	4	12,344	3	1
Canada (1989)	9,971	30.8	717	22,691	262	248
Chile (1994)	757	15.2	76	4,315	18	17
People's Republic of China (1991)	9,561	1,275.1	1,080	919	267	244
Hong Kong, China (1991)	1	6.9	162	24,080	177	205
Indonesia (1989)	1,904	212.1	152	676	66	37
Japan (1989)	378	127.1	4,765	37,299	403	349
Republic of Korea (1989)	99	46.7	462	8,918	150	141
Malaysia (1989)	333	22.2	90	3,891	90	76
Mexico (1993)	1,973	98.9	581	6,072	158	168
New Zealand (1989)	271	3.8	51	13,111	13	13
Papua New Guinea (1993)	463	4.8	4	620	3	1
Peru (1998)	1,285	25.7	54	2,051	7	7
Republic of the Philippines (1989)	300	75.7	75	926	35	36
Russia (1998)	17,075	145.5	260	2,147	95	44
Singapore (1989)	1	4.0	93	20,738	122	116
Chinese Taipei (1991)	36	22.2	309	12,599	122	107
Thailand (1989)	513	62.8	122	1,825	65	62
United States of America (1989)	9,373	283.2	9,825	35,401	731	1,180
Viet Nam (1998)	331	78.1	31	418	14	17

Area; Population
Source: The Economist: Pocket World in Figures: 2003 Edition
Current Price GDP; Current GDP per capita; Exports, fob; Imports, cif
Source: The APEC Regiona Trade and Investment 2002

THE APEC SECRETARIAT

To support APEC's expanding activities, Ministers established a secretariat in Singapore in February 1993.

The APEC Secretariat serves as the central link and core support mechanism for the APEC process providing coordination, technical and advisory support to member economies and APEC fora. It also performs a project management role, assisting fora and economies with the oversight of over 200 APEC-funded projects.

The Secretariat is also responsible for media and public relations for APEC and plays an important role in supporting APEC's external communications and outreach efforts as well as providing public affairs and media support to the host economy and APEC fora throughout the year. The Secretariat manages APEC's publishing program, maintains the main APEC website www.apecsec.org.sg which is the principal source of online information on APEC and operates the APEC Library as well as managing other APEC information resources and records.

The position of Executive Director of the Secretariat is at Ambassador level and is filled on secondment from the member economy chairing APEC that year. The Deputy Executive Director, who is from the economy next hosting APEC, takes over as Executive Director the following year. In 2001 the Executive Director is Ambassador Zhang Yan from the People's Republic of China and the Deputy Executive Director is Ambassador Alejandro de la Peña from Mexico. The Secretariat is staffed by professional officers seconded from APEC member economies and locally-recruited support staff.

APEC Secretariat Executive Director

Ambassador Piamsak was born in 1950 in Bangkok, Thailand. He was educated at Chulalongkorn University in Thailand and Wayne State University in the USA.

Ambassador Piamsak Milintachinda

His professional career is as follows:

1977 - 1980	Attache, Department of Economic Affairs Ministry of Foreign Affairs, Thailand
1981 - 1984	Second Secretary Royal Thai Embassy, Singapore
1985 - 1987	First Secretary, Department of ASEAN Affairs Ministry of Foreign Affairs, Thailand

1988 - 1991	Counsellor, Permanent Mission of Thailand to the United Nations, New York
1992 - 1994	Director, North American Division Department of American and South Pacific Affairs Ministry of Foreign Affairs, Thailand
1995 - 1999	Minister, Deputy Permanent Representative, Mission of Thailand to the World Trade Organization, Geneva
1999	Deputy Director-General, Department of ASEAN Affairs, Ministry of Foreign Affairs, Thailand
2000 - 2001	Deputy Director-General, Department of European Affairs, Ministry of Foreign Affairs, Thailand
2002	Ambassador, Deputy Executive Director Asia-Pacific Economic Cooperation Secretariat
1 Jan 2003	Ambassador, Executive Director Asia-Pacific Economic Cooperation Secretariat

He is married to Tarptip. They have two sons.

APEC Secretariat Deputy Executive Director

Ambassador Mario Artaza is the 11th Deputy Executive Director of the APEC Secretariat.

Born in Santiago, Chile, in 1937, Ambassador Artaza has a distinguished career in the Chilean and international public service and as an academic.

Ambassador Artaza joined the Chilean Ministry of Foreign Affairs in 1958 and was appointed to the Chilean Embassy in Washington, DC, in 1964.

Following the military coup in late 1973, Ambassador Artaza departed the service of the Chilean Government and joined the World Bank in 1974.

After being reinstated to the Chilean Government in 1990 Ambassador Artaza served in a number of senior posts including Ambassador to the United Kingdom and Ambassador to the United States.

Ambassador Artaza will serve as the Deputy Executive Director of the APEC Secretariat for the 2003 APEC year hosted by Thailand. Following established protocols Ambassador Artaza will be appointed the 12th Executive Director of the APEC Secretariat for the 2004 APEC year that is to be hosted by Chile.

Ambassador Mario Artaza

Ambassador Artaza's career details:

1958 - 1959	Legal Department, Chile Ministry of Foreign Affairs
1960 - 1963	Political Department, Ministry of Foreign Affairs
1964 - 1967	Third and Secons Secretary, Embassy of Chile in Washington, D.C
1968 - 1969	Assigned to the Chilean Delegation to the O.A.S as Second and First Secretary, and Member of the Chilean Delegation to the U.N. General Assembly
1969	Director and Professor of International Politics and International Organizations, Institute of Political Sciences, Catholic University of Chile (Sabbatical year)
1971 - 1973	Counselor, Embassy of Chile in Lima, Peru
1973	Charge d' Affaires, Embassy of Chile, Washington, D.C.
1974	Visiting Professor, University of the Pacific, California, & Visiting Fellow Overseas Development Council, Washington, D.C.
1974 - 1990	Country Officer for Pakistan, Argentina and Paraguay, and Senior Operations Officer for Latin America at the World Bank
1990 - 1992	Chilean Alternate Representative to the International Organizations in Switzerland
1992 - 1994	Director of Multilateral Policy, Chile Ministry of Foreign Affairs
1993 - 1995	Professor of the post-graduate course on International Organizations at the Institute of International Studies, University of Chile and at Diplomatic Academy
1994 - 1995	Director of the Policy Planning, Chile Ministry of Foreign Affairs
1996 - 1999	Ambassador of Chile to the United Kingdom
1999 - 2000	Ambassador of Chile to the United States
2000 - 2002	Director General of Foreign Policy, Ministry of Foreign Affairs
2003	Ambassador, Deputy Executive Director, Asia-Pacific Economic Cooperation Secretariat

COMMUNICATIONS AND PUBLIC AFFAIRS

The APEC Secretariat oversees media and public relations for APEC and disseminates information on APEC to targeted audiences and the public through a variety of means including an extensive publishing programme, websites and other electronic media, audio visual material, presentations, visitor briefings and outreach visits to APEC member economies. The Secretariat also plays an important role in providing public affairs and media support throughout the year to the host economy, other APEC member economies and APEC committees, working groups and other fora .

A major exercise underway is the implementation of a new APEC Communications and Outreach Strategy aimed at improving information delivery to key audiences and extending the reach of APEC communications efforts. The strategy focuses on developing greater understanding of APEC's role and agenda, as well as more widely promoting its achievements.

During 2002 the emphasis has been on putting in place centralised systems and staff resources to support a more extensive and proactive communications operation for APEC. A major accomplishment has been the establishment of an integrated and strengthened communications team at the APEC Secretariat. The new communications team will be able to provide a wide range of professional advice and services to APEC economies and fora and will work on the development of targeted communications strategies and outreach programmes for application across various sectors and economies.

Key Activities

- Implementation of a new communications and outreach strategy in consultation with members economies and APEC fora.
- Presentations delivered regularly to a wide variety of business, government and student groups.
- On-the-ground media liaison support to host economies of major APEC meetings and assistance in advance of and during key events to support coverage by international, regional and local media outlets.
- Issuing and dissemination of media releases and advisories regularly via email gateway and posted on the APEC website. Regular contact with journalists to encourage media coverage of key APEC events and activities.

- Production of a wide range of general information resources on APEC as part of the Secretariat's publishing programme and assistance with production of APEC fora publications.
- Sale of APEC publications and CD ROMS through sales/marketing agreements with book agents/distributors in Australia; Brunei Darussalam; Hong Kong, China; Malaysia; New Zealand; Singapore; USA and the United Kingdom. Monitoring of sales patterns to ensure electronic/hard-copy publishing combinations support information dissemination objectives and user needs.
- Major redevelopment underway of the APEC website to enhance functionalities and applications to support a more proactive web communications strategy. Revamping of the electronic Individual Action Plans (e-IAP) system to increase its user-friendliness and accessibility.
- Development of an APEC Projects Database to provide public access to comprehensive information on project activities undertaken by APEC and to provide a central reference for APEC fora to ascertain convergent or complementary projects being undertaken by others.
- Management and continuous improvement of APEC's document access policy to facilitate access to APEC records via electronic means.
- Provision of support to Mexico as APEC Chair for 2002 in implementing its outreach programmes.

Next Steps

The APEC Secretariat will continue to focus heavily on implementing a more proactive communications and outreach programme to more effectively publicise APEC's role and achievements and promote community input and engagement in APEC. The Secretariat will provide public affairs and media relations support to Mexico as APEC Chair for the remainder of 2002 and to Thailand as APEC Chair for 2003.

COMMUNICATIONS AND DATABASE SYSTEM

One of the mandates given by the APEC Ministers to the Secretariat is to establish direct and regular communications between the APEC Secretariat and APEC members, Lead Shepherds of Working Groups, and Committees. There is also a need to create an information repository at the APEC Secretariat to facilitate the movement and storage of APEC-related information. This information needs to be accessible to users in each member economy either in hard copy form or in electronic format.

The APEC website is one of the key management vehicles to fulfill the Secretariat's mandate. Users can access a wide range of information including the APEC calendar of events and documents from meetings on the APEC website at http://www.apecsec.org.sg.

Achievements

- E-mail has become the major communication tool within APEC. All APEC member economies, working groups, committees and the business/private sector can easily communicate with the Secretariat by e-mail. Users can also access selected APEC documents through the APEC Secretariat's homepage.
- The contents of the Secretariat's website are updated frequently and more business-related linkages have been created.

HOW APEC OPERATES

Ministerial and Senior Officials' Meetings

APEC operates by consensus. In 1991, members committed themselves to conducting their activities and work programs on the basis of open dialogue with equal respect for the views of all participants. The APEC Chair, which rotates annually among members, is responsible for hosting the annual ministerial meeting of foreign and economic ministers. The People's Republic of China is the APEC Chair for 2001.

In addition to the annual APEC Ministerial Meeting, APEC member economies have hosted a number of other ministerial-level meetings in the following areas: education, energy, environment and sustainable development, finance, human resources development (HRD), regional science and technology cooperation, small and medium enterprises, telecommunications and information industry, trade, transportation, and women.

APEC Senior Officials' Meetings (SOM) are held regularly prior to every ministerial meeting. The SOM makes recommendations to the Ministers and carries out their decisions. It oversees and coordinates, with approval from Ministers, the budgets and work programs of the APEC fora.

APEC in Action/APEC Fora

At each year's Ministerial Meeting, members define and fund work programs for APEC's three committees, one sub-committee, 11 working groups and other APEC fora.

In 1993 APEC Ministers adopted a Declaration on a Trade and Investment Framework to increase economic activity and facilitate the flow of goods and services among member economies. Based on the Declaration, Ministers formed the *Committee on Trade and Investment (CTI).* The CTI aims to create an APEC perspective on trade and investment issues and to pursue liberalization and facilitation initiatives. The CTI is responsible to senior officials for coordinating and implementing the liberalization and facilitation components of the Osaka Action Agenda, [ital removed] including work on tariffs, non-tariff measures, services, deregulation, dispute mediation, implementation of WTO obligations, investment, customs procedures, standards and conformance, mobility of business people, intellectual property rights, competition policy, government procurement and rules of origin. Activities in these areas are undertaken by the sub-committees and experts' group established under the CTI. The CTI, whose current chair is the United States of America, also played a key role in APEC's development of initiatives for EVSL, review of the IAP process and work to "strengthen markets".

In 2001, the CTI will, in addition to progressing its core activity of implementation and enhancement of the Collective Action Plans (CAPs), be responsible for the review and development of the OAA for use by member economies to show how they intend to achieve Bogor *[ital removed]* goals and development of a set of non-binding Principles on Trade Facilitation. The CTI will also oversee the implementation of the APEC Strategic Plan on Capacity Building related to the Implementation of WTO Agreements and Cooperation Framework for Strengthening Economic Legal Infrastructure.

The *Economic Committee (EC)* was established by APEC Ministers in November 1994. The EC analyzes economic trends and issues in support of APEC's trade and investment liberalization and facilitation and economic and technical cooperation agendas. The EC presented three major published reports to the Ministerial meeting in November 2000 in Brunei Darussalam, namely: *2000 APEC Economic Outlook*, *APEC Economies beyond the Asian Crisis*, and *Towards Knowledge-based Economies in APEC.*

The *2001 APEC Economic Outlook*, which is being coordinated by Hong Kong, China, will analyze the nexus between financial development and economic growth. This year the EC will also undertake a major research project that will study the issues and policy challenges relating to the New Economy.

The *Budget and Management Committee (BMC)* advises APEC Senior Officials on budgetary, administrative and managerial issues. It assesses and makes recommendations on the budget structure, considers budget requests, drafts the annual APEC budget and examines all questions relating to the APEC budget and budgetary process. In addition, it is empowered by the Senior Officials to monitor and evaluate the operations and overall performance of working groups and make recommendations to the SOM for improved efficiency and effectiveness. The committee holds two regular meetings each year.

The ECOTECH Sub-Committee of the SOM (ESC) was established in 1998 to assist the SOM in coordinating and managing APEC's economic and technical cooperation (ECOTECH) agenda and identifying value-added initiatives for cooperative action. The ESC seeks to advance effective implementation of Part II of the 1995 Osaka Action Agenda, the 1996 Manila Framework for Strengthening Economic Cooperation and Development and other ECOTECH initiatives through consultation with APEC fora and the development of policy management tools and guidelines for projects.

This year, the ESC will develop further the Joint Activities/Dialogue sections of Part II of the Osaka Action Agenda, coordinate work on cross-cutting issues, consider the possibility of establishing Individual Action Plans on ECOTECH and report on the implementation of ECOTECH guidelines and initiatives. The ESC will lead a special coordinating group of HRD representatives, established to develop a human capacity building strategy that would define the objectives, priorities and principles for enabling APEC to respond to the challenges of the new economy. It will also contribute to APEC's outreach programs by highlighting how ECOTECH activities are benefiting member economy governments, the business/private sector and the community.

Following a decision by Ministers in 1999, the Infrastructure Workshop has been re-constituted as the *Group on Economic Infrastructure (GEI)* under the ESC. The GEI will continue to utilize the Public-Private/Business Sector Dialogue process, the "Economic Regulation and Creditworthiness Enhancement" work and the Regional Integration for Sustainable Economies (RISE) initiative to make available to member economies the lessons learnt and best practices in support of policies and frameworks for the provision of infrastructure services. It will also review infrastructure support work undertaken in other fora, notably that relating to sustainable urban development, in order to assess APEC's future role in this field.

The Ad Hoc Policy Level Group on Small and Medium Enterprises (PLGSME), was established in 1995. As a result of the management review, the SOM decided to rename it as the *Small and Medium Enterprises Working Group (SME).* The SME oversees activities for SMEs across all APEC fora. There is a consensus in APEC that free trade and economic globalization have implications, challenges and opportunities for SMEs. In 2001, the SME Ministerial Meeting will be held on 29-31 August, in Shanghai, in parallel with the Business Forum, and a joint session will again be held between the Ministerial Meeting and the Business Forum. On the margins of both meetings, an SMEs Achievements Exhibition will be held.

The APEC *Energy Working Group (EWG)* was established in 1990 and obtained its current mandate in 1995 from APEC Ministers and Leaders to implement the energy work program contained in the Osaka Action Agenda[ital removed]. The EWG pursues its objectives through projects undertaken by the Asia Pacific Energy Research Centre and by expert groups on: clean fossil energy; new and renewable energy technologies; mineral and energy exploration and development; energy data and analysis; energy efficiency and conservation; and the energy regulators' forum. [caps removed]

Energy Ministers met for the fourth time in 2000 in San Diego, to discuss regional energy cooperation and the role of energy in meeting APEC's goals in the 21st century. In their Declaration, Energy Ministers committed themselves to the implementation of priority energy initiatives on a voluntary basis. These initiatives include strategies to enhance energy efficiency and conservation; and disseminate new and renewable energy technologies that would facilitate energy security and regional economic stability.

The *Fisheries Working Group (FWG)*, established in 1991, aims to maximize the economic benefits and sustainability of fisheries resources for all APEC members. Its work complements and contributes to the work of other international and regional fisheries organizations in the Pacific and has related to compliance issues and coordination based on member economy inspection systems, standards, and other requirements aimed at improved seafood inspection regimes in APEC member economies. The working group has been conducting a four-year study of fisheries sector trade and investment liberalization in the areas of tariffs, non-tariff measures, investment measures, and subsidies.

The *Human Resources Development Working Group (HRD),* established in 1990, is driven by its goal of promoting the well-being of all people in the region through economic growth and development. The working group streamlined its structure in 2000 and reduced its original five networks to three, focusing on capacity building, education, and labour and social protection.

In 2001 the HRD will continue to focus on contributing towards HRD and human capacity building efforts. In addition to pursuing its work program the working group aims to contribute to the development of an APEC-wide human capacity building strategy. It will be working for a successful outcome of the APEC High Level Meeting on Human Capacity Building in Beijing, on 15-16 May 2001, and the fourth Human Resources Development Ministerial Meeting in Kumamoto, on 29-30 September 2001.

The *Industrial Science and Technology Working Group (IST)*, set up in 1990, has recently updated its Action Program to focus on two major initiatives, the APEC Agenda for Science and Technology Cooperation into the 21st Century, and Harnessing Technology for the Future. The 21st century agenda was endorsed by the Leaders at their meeting in Kuala Lumpur in 1998 and the harnessing technology initiative was adopted by the Ministers in Manila in 1996, as one of the six themes for economic and technical cooperation. The harnessing technology initiative has six priorities: improved availability of information; improved human resources development; improved business climate; contribution to sustainable development; enhanced policy dialogue and review; and facilitation of networks and partnership. The IST has been actively implementing many projects under these themes.

The IST has contributed to the APEC goal of sustainable development through the development, in 1997, of the Cleaner Production Strategy and, in early 1998, of an APEC action plan on infectious diseases. In 2001 the IST will further develop its strategy to fight infectious diseases as requested by APEC Leaders at their meeting in 2000.

The *Marine Resource Conservation Working Group (MRC)* was formed in 1990 in recognition of the importance of marine resources to food supply and economic development. The MRC is committed to promoting the sustainability of the marine environment within the APEC Region to ensure continuing socio-economic and environmental benefits. In 2001, the group plans to work on a wide range of issues: the management of red tide and harmful algal bloom; the establishment of an ocean research network and an ocean model and information system; the use of biochemical indicators to assess environmental safety of aquaculture farms; and the development of APEC mechanisms for integrated coastal management. These activities will contribute to capacity building, training and education, the exchange of information, research promotion, and the introduction of technology and expertise. The MRC is also seeking to establish partnerships with the private sector, and to publicize success stories of public-private partnerships or private industries' efforts in enhancing marine environment protection.

The *Telecommunications and Information Working Group (TEL)* was formed in 1990 to address: human resource development; technology transfer and regional cooperation; and telecommunications standardization. The 1995 Seoul Declaration on an Asia Pacific Information Infrastructure (APII), adopted at the first APEC Ministerial Meeting on Telecommunications and Information, contains ten core principles aimed at facilitating trade and investment. At the fourth Ministerial Meeting in May 2000 in Mexico, the working group was directed to strengthen the APII, as well as to implement the Reference Framework for Action on Electronic Commerce and the APEC Blueprint for Action on Electronic Commerce. Ministers emphasized the need to promote a pro-competitive environment that will enhance the development of telecommunications and the information infrastructure. Ministers also emphasized the need to bridge the digital divide and enhance reliable and affordable access to the information infrastructure. In response, the working group has developed a *Digital Divide Blueprint for Action.* The Blueprint is an attempt to provide a cohesive plan of action for the TEL to focus and coordinate the activities of its four steering groups to address the issue of the digital divide.

The *Tourism Working Group (TWG)* was formed in 1991 based on the recognition that the tourism industry is of growing importance in promoting economic growth and social development in the Asia-Pacific region. The TWG brings together tourism administrators to share information, exchange views and develop areas of cooperation on trade and policies.

The Seoul Declaration on an APEC Tourism Charter was adopted by APEC Tourism Ministers during their first Ministerial Meeting held on 5-7 July 2000 in Seoul. It recognizes the significant contribution tourism makes to APEC economies and reflects a collective commitment to improve the economic, cultural, social and environmental well being of APEC member economies through tourism. The Seoul Declaration on an APEC Tourism Charter includes measures that:

- will remove impediments to tourism business and investment;
- will increase mobility of visitors and demand for tourism goods and services in the APEC Region;
- sustainably manage tourism outcomes and impacts;
- enhance recognition and understanding of tourism as a vehicle for economic and social development; and

- take into account the "Framework for the Integration of Women in APEC".

The policy goals and processes adopted in the Charter are consistent with the goals for free and open trade and investment established in the *Bogor Declaration* and the general principles for trade liberalization and economic and technical cooperation established in the Osaka Action Agenda.

During its last meeting in Melaka the TWG endorsed an APEC/Pacific Asia Travel Association Code for Sustainable Tourism. The Second APEC Tourism Forum was held in April 2001 in Kuala Lumpur. The Second APEC Tourism Ministerial Meeting will be hosted in Manzanillo, in July 2002.

The *Trade Promotion Working Group (TP)* first met in Seoul in June 1990. Its work centers on trade promotion activities, trade financing, trade skills and training, trade information and networking, and cooperation between the private sector and public agencies, including trade promotion organizations. The TP has provided the business community with information through APEC-Net and publication of an APEC Trade-Show Directory, and held a venture capital workshop and a seminar on credit guarantee systems to exchange views on trade financing. It demonstrates its interest in business engagement through the APEC International Trade Fair and the Asia-Pacific Business Network and its meeting back-to-back with the meetings of the APEC Trade Promotion Organization.

The *Transportation Working Group (TPT)* was established in 1991 with a view to increasing the efficiency and safety of the regional transportation system. It has conducted important initiatives of trade facilitation as well as projects in close cooperation with the business/private sector. The group's Road Transportation Harmonization Project will provide the basis for standards harmonization in the automotive sector in the Asia-Pacific region. The TPT focuses on three main areas: more competitive transportation industry (including infrastructure), safe and environment-friendly transportation systems (including technologies), and human resources development (including training, research and education). Covering all types of transportation systems, the group has published surveys, directories, best practice manuals and databases, as well as an inventory on regional cooperation on oil-spills preparedness and response arrangements. Transportation Ministers met in Washington, D.C. in June 1995 and in Victoria, B.C., in June 1997 and will next meet in October 2001 in Peru.

The Agricultural Technical Cooperation Experts Group was established as a formal APEC body in 1996 and renamed as *Agricultural Technical Cooperation Working Group (ATC)* at the Ministerial Meeting in 2000. By strengthening agricultural technical cooperation, APEC economies are seeking to enhance the capability of agriculture and its related industries to contribute to economic growth and social well-being. The priority areas for the ATC are: conservation and utilization of plant and animal genetic resources; research, development and extension of agricultural biotechnology; production, processing, marketing, distribution and consumption of agricultural products; plant and animal quarantine and pest management; agricultural finance systems; agricultural technology transfer and training; and sustainable agriculture and related environmental issues.

At Blake Island in 1993 APEC Economic Leaders gave a call to action to APEC members to manage their resources in such a way as to ensure that growth takes sustainability into consideration. APEC addresses *environment/sustainable development* as a cross-cutting issue that should be addressed by all APEC fora. Based on the outcomes of the two previous APEC Environmental Ministers' Meetings (in Manila, 1996 and Toronto, 1997), APEC Ministers and Leaders in November 1998 in Kuala Lumpur outlined the priorities on sustainable development in five areas. They are: cleaner production; protection of the marine environment; sustainable cities; food, energy, and the environment in relation to economic and population growth (FEEEP); and the APEC Framework for Capacity Building Initiatives on Emergency Preparedness.

In 1997 APEC Economic Leaders made the commitment to integrate gender issues into the mainstream of APEC activities. As part of the commitment, the first APEC Ministerial Meeting on Women was held in Manila, 15-16 October 1998. The meeting made recommendations on how APEC should put in to operation the commitment to integrate women in its activities embodied in the Framework for the Integration of Women in APEC in 1999. Following this, the SOM Ad-Hoc Advisory Group for Gender Integration (AGGI) was formed to provide gender advice and expertise to the SOM and other APEC fora on the implementation of the Framework. The AGGI holds gender information sessions (GIS) for APEC fora. To date, GIS have been undertaken by 19 APEC fora, including the SOM and the APEC Secretariat. The AGGI has also developed gender criteria for use in APEC project proposals and approval and evaluation reports. It has also been overseeing the compilation of good practices of gender integration in APEC fora and economies. To complement the four critical tasks, the AGGI is also undertaking a sex-disaggregated data project. Meanwhile, it is also developing practical strategies that will further integrate gender issues into the APEC process.

Management Review

A three-year management review of the APEC process was completed in 2000. Following the achievements in 1998 and 1999, additional measures to increase the efficiency and effectiveness of the APEC process were endorsed and taken by both the Senior Officials and the Ministers in 2000. The major measures were:

- Adoption of criteria for the establishment of new APEC fora,
- Adoption of mechanisms for developing greater links with APEC Financial Ministers' process, and
- Redesignation of: the PLGSME as the Small and Medium Enterprises Working Group; ATC as the Agricultural Technical Cooperation Working Group; and the Infrastructure Workshop as the Group on Economic Infrastructure.
- While the three-year management review program has been concluded successfully, APEC will continue its efforts to streamline the APEC process.

APEC OBJECTIVES

The member economies represent the rich diversity of the region as well as differing levels of economic development. Despite such differences there is a growing sense of common purpose and cooperation aimed at sustained regional and world growth.

APEC has come a long way since 1989. It has built steadily on the efforts of the past and looks forward to further progress. The initial years of APEC were focused largely on exchanges of views and project-based initiatives. The concerns were simply to advance the process of Asia-Pacific economic cooperation and to promote a positive conclusion to the Uruguay Round of GATT negotiations.

Informal Leaders' Meetings are held annually since 1993, with each meeting resulting in significant initiatives and action plans:

Blake Island, 1993

APEC Economic Leaders met for the first time in November, 1993, when they held informal discussions at Blake Island near Seattle. They envisioned a community of Asia-Pacific economies, based on the spirit of openness and partnership; which would make cooperative efforts to address the challenges of: change; promote the free exchange of goods, services and investment; and work towards broadly-based economic growth, higher living and educational standards and sustainable growth that respects the natural environment.

In subsequent annual meetings, APEC Ministers and Leaders further refined this vision and launched mechanisms to translate it into action. In 1994 in Bogor, the vision of an open trading system became the very ambitious goal of "*free and open trade and investment in the Asia-Pacific by 2010 for developed member economies and 2020 for developing ones*".

Bogor, 1994

APEC envisioned "free and open trade and investment in the Asia-Pacific by 2010 for developed member economies and 2020 for developing ones".

Osaka, 1995

In Osaka, APEC Leaders adopted the Osaka Action Agenda (OAA), which firmly established the three pillars of APEC activities: trade and investment liberalization, business facilitation, and economic and technical cooperation.

Manila, 1996

The Manila Action Plan for APEC (MAPA), adopted by the APEC Leaders in November 1996, compiled members' initial individual action plans to achieve the objectives outlined in Bogor. APEC Leaders also instructed that high priority be given to the following six areas of economic and technical cooperation: developing human capital; fostering safe and efficient capital markets; strengthening economic infrastructure; harnessing technologies of the future; promoting environmentally sustainable growth; and encouraging the growth of small and medium-sized enterprises.

Vancouver, 1997

In Vancouver APEC Leaders recognized members' efforts to improve the commitments in their Individual Action Plans (IAPs) and reaffirmed their intention to update these annually. APEC Leaders endorsed their Ministers' agreement that action should be taken with respect to early voluntary sectoral liberalization (EVSL) in 15 sectors, with nine to be advanced throughout 1998 and implementation to begin in 1999. APEC Leaders welcomed the progress of APEC fora in involving business, academics and other experts, women and youth and encouraged them to continue these efforts. APEC Leaders endorsed the Vancouver Framework for Enhanced Public-Private Partnership for Infrastructure Development.

Kuala Lumpur, 1998

In Kuala Lumpur APEC Leaders reaffirmed their confidence in the strong economic fundamentals and prospects for recovery of the economies of the Asia-Pacific. They agreed to pursue a cooperative growth strategy to end the financial crisis. They pledged efforts to strengthen: social safety nets; financial systems; trade and investment flows; the scientific and technological base; human resources development; economic infrastructure; and business and commercial links, so as to provide the base and set the pace for sustained growth into the 21st century. APEC Leaders also welcomed the Ministers' decision to seek an EVSL agreement with non-APEC members at the World Trade Organisation.

The APEC Leaders adopted the Kuala Lumpur Action Program on Skills Development with the objective of contributing towards sustainable growth and equitable development while reducing economic disparities and improving the social well-being of the people, through skills upgrading/improvement.

Auckland, 1999

At their meeting in September 1999 in Auckland, APEC Leaders agreed that the performance and prospects of the APEC economies had improved, but they were not complacent about the risks to recovery. Accordingly they pledged to strengthen markets and improve the international framework governing trade and investment flows. APEC Leaders also put people and their prosperity at the forefront of their discussions, welcoming the more active participation of women and the business sector in APEC's work.

BUSINESS/PRIVATE SECTOR INVOLVEMENT

Key features that set APEC apart from other international organizations are its commitment to facilitating business and that it regularly brings the business/private sector into a wide range of APEC activities. Business has always been the primary force behind the dynamic growth in the Asia-Pacific region and the continuing globalization of business means that the APEC economies must develop region-wide practices and policies to encourage the free flow of goods, services, investment and capital within the region. Therefore business is a key constituency for APEC both regionally and in individual member economies. APEC aims to achieve both concrete and pragmatic results that will benefit business, contribute to increased income and create jobs in the region.

Recognizing that business expertise and resources can help APEC achieve its objectives, the business/private sector already participates in many of APEC's working groups and helps shape the policy dialogue in partnership with member economy officials. APEC Economic Leaders receive advice from the APEC Business Advisory Council (ABAC) established in late 1995. Such involvement is important, ensuring that APEC's work addresses real problems and proposes practical solutions and a major APEC goal is to continue to expand the essential role of business in the APEC process.

APEC Business Advisory Council

In 1995 APEC Economic Leaders established a permanent council composed of up to three senior business people from each member economy to provide advice on the implementation of APEC action plans and on other specific business/private sector priorities. Chairmanship of ABAC rotates each year according to which economy chairs APEC. The 2001 ABAC Chair is Mr Qin Xiao, Vice Chairman of the China International Trust and Investment Corporation of the People's Republic of China.

ABAC has presented five published reports to APEC Leaders on the theme of "APEC Means Business," containing specific recommendations for improving regional business conditions and expanding trade and investment. ABAC's 2000 report focused on proposals to help APEC member economies stay on track with trade and investment liberalization and facilitation, build stronger financial systems, and improve access to new opportunities through technological progress. Specific ABAC recommendations targeted: the growing issue of non-tariff measures; implementing an APEC food system; promoting business mobility; removing impediments to standards and conformance; developing bond markets and an Institute of Directors Network; developing action plans for e-commerce; and harnessing the Internet for human resources development. ABAC members have the opportunity to discuss their recommendations at their annual dialogue with APEC Leaders and at various ministerial meetings throughout the year.

APEC Activities in 2000

With the emerging signs of economic recovery in the region, APEC Economic Leaders, in their meeting in Bandar Seri Begawan in November 2000, mapped out ways of preserving, strengthening and further opening markets as well as sustaining economic recovery in APEC. Aiming to deliver on the various agreements, to the people and the diverse communities that APEC serves, they decided to address the challenges of the New Economy in the following areas:

Managing Globalization.

APEC Leaders directed their Ministers to reinvigorate APEC's programs in economic and technical cooperation and to continue to work in international forums to help shape the global economy and provide a more secure and stable financial environment.

The Action Agenda for the New Economy.

This agenda brings together all of the elements related to the New Economy that APEC has been working on for some time: the e-Commerce Readiness Assessment, paperless trading, and building capacity in both people and institutions. APEC Leaders instructed their Ministers to expand and develop the agenda to create an environment for strengthening: market structures, institutions and infrastructure investment, technology development ; and building both human capacity and entrepreneurship development.

Creating New Opportunities.

APEC Leaders committed themselves to working to ensure all people of urban, provincial, and rural communities in every APEC member economy have individual or community-based access to the information and services offered by the Internet by 2010. As a first step, APEC Leaders pledged to triple the number of people within the APEC region with such access by 2005.

Strengthening the Multilateral Trading System.

APEC Leaders reiterated the need to expeditiously launch a new WTO round. They agreed that a balanced and broad-based agenda responding to the interests and concerns of all WTO members should be formalized and finalized as soon as possible in 2001 and that a round be launched in 2001.

Making APEC Matter More

In addition to urging APEC to expand its work in outreach, APEC Leaders instructed their Ministers to ensure that the new "electronic-Individual Action Plans" be fully operational in 2001 and updated and improved as an electronic tool in future years. (These IAPs are the basic road maps by which each APEC member charts its progress toward the Bogor goals of trade and investment liberalization. The new electronic version has greatly enhanced their accessibility and usefulness for business.)

ACRONYMS

AASE	APEC Association of Stock Exchanges
ABAC	APEC Business Advisory Council
ABTC	APEC Business Travel Card
ACDS	APEC Communications and Database System
ACEN	APEC Cyber Education Network
ACI	Airports Council International for Pacific Region
ACTETSME	APEC Center for Technology Exchange and Training for Small and Medium Enterprises
ADB	Asian Development Bank
AEEMTRC	ASEAN-EC Energy Management Training and Research Centre
AEF	APEC Education Foundation
AEM	APEC Education Ministers
AEMC	ASEAN-EC Management Centre
AEMM	APEC Education Ministers Meeting
AFG	APEC Financiers' Group
AFMM	APEC Finance Ministers Meeting
AFS	APEC Food System
AFTA	ASEAN Free Trade Area
AGGI	Advisory Group on Gender Integration
AIFN	APEC Infrastructure Facilitation Network
AIMS	APEC Impediments Measurement Systems
AIRIC	APEC Infrastructure Resource Integration Centre
ALEI	APEC Leaders' Education Initiative
AMETEC	APEC Marine Environmental Training and Education Center
AMM	APEC Ministerial Meeting
ANSC	APEC National Study Center, Korea
ANZCERTA	Australia New Zealand Closer Economic Relations Trade Agreement
AOEMA	Asia Oceania Electronic Marketplace Association
AOMM	APEC Ocean-Related Ministerial Meeting
APB-Net	Asia-Pacific Business Network
APEC	Asia-Pacific Economic Cooperation
APERC	Asia Pacific Energy Research Center
APG	Asia Pacific Group on Money Laundering
APIAN	APEC International Assessment Network
APII	Asia-Pacific Information Infrastructure
APIS	Asia-Pacific Information
APLAC	Asia Pacific Laboratory Accreditation Co-operation

APLMF	Asia Pacific Legal Metrology Forum
APMP	Asia Pacific Metrology Program
APRCP	Asia Pacific Roundtable on Cleaner Production
APT	Asia Pacific Telecommunity
ASCC	APEC Study Centers Consortium
ASEAN	Association of South-East Asian Nations *(Includes Brunei Darussalam, Cambodia, Indonesia, Laos, Malaysia, Myanmar, the Philippines, Singapore, Thailand and Viet Nam)*
ASEF	Asia-Europe Foundation
AST	APEC Science and Technology
ATC	Agricultural Technical Cooperation Working Group *(formerly was ATCEG)*
ATCEG	Agricultural Technical Cooperation Experts' Group *(now known as ATCWG)*
ATL	Accelerated Tariff Liberalization
AVIP	APEC Voluntary Investment Project
B2G	Business to Government
BAC	Budget and Administrative Committee *(now known as BMC)*
BERI	Business Environment Risk Intelligence (based in Washington)
BMC	Budget and Management Committee *(formerly was BAC)*
BMEG	Experts Group on Business Mobility
BMN	Business Management Network
BVP	Business Volunteers Program
CAP	Collective Action Plans
CBN	Capacity Building Network
CEPAL	Economic Commission for Latin America (in Santiago)
CEPI	Consumer Education and Protection Initiative
CEPT	Common Effective Preferential Tariff (Under ASEAN)
CER	Closer Economic Relations
CITEL	Inter-American Telecommunication Commission
CNBC	Mexican National Business Council
CODEX	Codex Alimentarius Commission
COW	Committee of the Whole
CRAs	Credit Rating Agencies
CSIS	Centre for Strategic and International Studies
CTI	Committee on Trade and Investment
DDA	Doha Development Agenda
DMEG	Dispute Mediation Experts' Group
EBN	EWG Business Network
EC	Economic Committee
ECOTECH	Economic and Technical Cooperation

ECSG	Electronic Commerce Steering Group
EdFor	APEC Education Forum
EDI	Electronic Data Interchange
EDNET	Education Network
EDZ	Economic Development Zone
EFIs	Export Financing Institutions
E-FITS	APEC Working Group on Electronic Financial Transaction Systems
EGMS	Experts Group on Maritime Safety (under TPT)
EGNRET	EWG Expert Group on New and Renewable Energy Technologies
e-IAP	Electronic Individual Action Plan
EID	Emerging Infectious Diseases
EMEAP	Executive Meeting of East Asian and Pacific Central Banks
EPG	Eminent Persons Group
ERF	Energy Regulators' Forum
ESC	ECOTECH Sub-Committee of the SOM
ESCAP	Economic and Social Commission for Asia and the Pacific
ESI	Econ. Strategy Int.
ETI	Economic Trends and Issues Ad Hoc Group
EU	European Union
EVSL	Early Voluntary Sectoral Liberalization
EWG	Energy Working Group
FACTS	Facilitation, Accountability, Consistency, Transparency and Simplification
FAO	Food and Agriculture Organization
FATF	Financial Action Task Force on Money Laundering
FDI	Foreign Direct Investment
FEEEP	Food, Energy, Environment, Economic Development and Population
FIC	Forum Island Countries
FIN	Finance Working Group (APEC Finance Ministers Process)
FOB	Free on Board
FSAP	Financial Sector Assessment Program (by IMF/World Bank)
FSF	Financial Stability Forum
FTA	Free Trade Agreement
FTAA	Free Trade Area of the Americas
FWG	Fisheries Working Group
G-8	Group of Eight *(Includes United States, Japan, Germany, France, Italy, United Kingdom Canada and Russia)*
GAC	Government Advisory Committee

GATS	General Agreement on Trade in Services
GATT	General Agreement on Tariffs and Trade
GBD	Global Business Dialogue
GBDe	Global Business Dialogue on Electronic Commerce
GDP	Gross Domestic Product
GEI	Group on Economic Infrastructure *(formerly was IWS)*
GIN	G-7 Global Information Network
GIS	Global Information Society
GIS	Gender Information Sessions
GNSS	Global Navigation Satellite Systems
GOS	Group on Services
GP	Government Procurement
GPA	Global Programme of Action
GPEG	Government Procurement Experts' Group
GPS	Global Positioning System
GSP	Generalised System of Preferences
GSTP	Global System of Trade Preference
HACCP	Hazard Analysis and Critical Control Points
HCB	Human Capacity Building
HCBCG	Human Capacity Building Coordinating Group
HRD	Human Resources Development Working Group
HURDIT	HRD in Industrial Technology Network
IADB	Inter-American Development Bank
IAIS	International Association of Insurance Supervisors
IAP	Individual Action Plan
ICAIS	International Charging Arrangements for Internet Services
ICANN	Internet Corporation for Assigned Names and Numbers
ICAO	International Civil Aviation Organization
ICC	International Chamber of Commerce
ICFA	International Coalition of Fisheries Association
ICSID	International Convention on the Settlement of Investment Disputes
ICT	Information and Communication Technology
IDE	Institute of Developing Economies
IDEAS	Institute of Developing Economies Advance School, Japan
IEA	International Energy Agency
IEA	International Association for the Evaluation of Educational Achievement
IEC	International Electrotechnical Commission
IEG	Investment Experts' Group
IFAT	Implementation Facilitation Assistance Team

IFIs	International Financial Institutions
IIE	Institute for International Economics (in the US)
III	Infrastructure Investment Initiative
ILO	International Labour Organisation
IMD	International Institute for Management Development
IMF	International Monetary Fund
IMO	International Maritime Organization
IMTA	International Transport Association
INCPEC	Indonesian National Committee for Pacific Economic Cooperation
INDECOPI	National Institute for the Defense of Competition and Protection of Intellectual Property
INGECEP	Integrated Next Generation Electronic Commerce Environment Project (Under TEL)
INTA	International Trademark Association
IOSCO	International Organization of Securities Commissions
IPEG	Intellectual Property Rights Experts Group
IPP	Independent Power Producer
IPR	Intellectual Property Rights
IQAS	International Quality Assurance Systems
ISO	International Organization for Standardization
ISO9000	International Standards Organization: 9000
ISTWG	Industrial Science and Technology Working Group
IT	Information Technology
ITA	Information Technology Agreement
ITS	Intelligent Transport Systems
ITU	International Telecommunication Union
IUU	Illegal, Unregulated and Unreported
IVANS	International Value Added Network Services
IWS	Infrastructure Workshop *(now known as GEI)*
JETRO	Japan External Trade Organization
KBE	Knowledge-based Economy
KIEP	Korea Institute of International Economic Policy
LAIA	Latin American Integration Association
LCA	Life Cycle Assessment
LMI	Labour Market Information
LNG	Liquefied Natural Gas
MAG	Market Access Group
MAPA	Manila Action Plan for APEC
MDBs	Multilateral Development Banks
MEF	Minerals and Energy Forum

MERCOSUR	Mercado Comun del Cono Sur (Southern Cone Common Market)
MFN	Most Favoured Nation
MI	Maritime Initiative
MNE	Multinational Enterprise
MRA	Mutual Recognition Arrangement
MRC	Marine Resource Conservation Working Group
MRT	Ministers Responsible for Trade
NAFTA	North American Free Trade Agreement
NAPs	Network Access Points
NATO	North Atlantic Treaty Organization
NBIP	Non-Binding Investment Principles
NEDA	National Economic and Development Authority
NEDM	Economic Development Management Network
NGO	Non-Governmental Organization
NPL	Non-Performing Loan
NTM	Non-Tariff Measures
OAA	Osaka Action Agenda
OAS	Organization of American States
OECD	Organization for Economic Cooperation and Development
OFC	Offshore Financial Center
OIML	Organisation Internationale De Metrologie Legale
OMISAR	Ocean Model and Information System
ORNEP	Ocean Research Network for the Pacific
PAC	Pacific Accreditation Cooperation
PAFTAD	Pacific Trade and Development Conference
PAQPM	Plant and Animal Quarantine and Pest Management
PASC	Pacific Area Standards Congress
PATA	Pacific Asia Travel Association
PBEC	Pacific Basin Economic Council
PECC	Pacific Economic Cooperation Council
PBF	Pacific Business Forum
PEG	Partnership for Equitable Growth
PEG	Port Experts Group (under TPT)
PEO	Pacific Economic Outlook
PFP	Partners for Progress
PIF	Pacific Islands Forum *(formerly was SPF)*
PLG	Policy Level Group
PLGSME	Policy Level Group on Small and Medium Enterprises *(now known as SMEWG)*
PTA	Preferential Trading Agreements
R & A	Research and Analysis

R & D	Research & Development
REC	Regional Energy Cooperation
REDAP	Peruvian Network for Asia Pacific Studies
RFMO	Regional Fisheries Management Organization
RGC	Regional Growth Center
RISE	Regional Integration for Sustainable Economies
ROO	Rules of Origin
ROSC	Reports on Observance of Standards and Codes
RTA	Regional Trade Agreement
S & T	Science and Technology
SAL	Structural Adjustment Loans
SCCP	Sub-Committee on Customs Procedures
SCSC	Sub-Committee on Standards and Conformance
SDCs	Skill Development Centers
SEACEN	South East Asian Central Banks Research and Training Center
SEAMEO	Southeast Asian Ministers of Education Organization
SELI	Strengthening Economic Legal Infrastructure SGES Steering Group on Energy Standards
SIS	Seafood Information Systems
SME	Small and Medium Enterprises Working Group *(formerly was PLGSME)*
SMTEs	Small & Medium Tourism Enterprises
SOM	Senior Officials' Meeting
SPAN	Integrated Plan of Action for SME Development
SPARTECA	South Pacific Regional Trade & Economic Cooperation Agreement
SPF	South Pacific Forum *(now known as PIF)*
SPS	Sanitary and Phytosanitary Measures
SRB	Specialist Regional Body
SRTA	Subregional Trading Arrangements
SSN	Social Safety Nets
SSOM	Special Senior Officials Meeting
STI	IMF-Singapore Regional Training Institute
STIP	Science & Technology Industrial Park
TBT	Technical Barriers to Trade
TDB	APEC Tariff Database
TEL	Telecommunications and Information Working Group *(formerly was Telecommunications Working Group)*
TELMIN	Ministerial Meeting on Telecommunications and Information Industries
TFF	Task Force on Food

TFMI	Task Force on Management Issues
TFTF	Task Force on Trade Facilitation
TID	Trade and Investment Data Review Working Group
TIDDB	Trade and Investment Data Database
TIDWG	Trade and Investment Data Review Working Group
TIITP	Trade and Investment Insurance Training Program
TILF	Trade and Investment Liberalization and Facilitation
TIN	Tourism Information Network
TMM	Trade Ministers Meeting
TNDC	Trade Negotiation among Developing Countries
TOB	Tender Offer Bid
TP	Trade Promotion Working Group
TPO	Trade Promotion Organisations
TPT	Transportation Working Group
TQM	Total Quality Management
TRIMS	Trade-related Investment Measures
TRIPS	Trade-Related Aspects of Intellectual Property Rights
TSA	Tourism Satellite Accounts (under TWG)
TSAT	Trade Skills on Training
TTA	Training and Technical Assistance
TWG	Tourism Working Group
UMAP	University Mobility in Asia and the Pacific
UN	United Nations
UN/EDIFACT	United Nations Rules for Electronic Data Interchange for Administration, Commerce and Transport
UNCED	United Nations Conference on Environment and Development
UNCITRAL	United Nations Commission on International Trade Law
UNCTAD	United Nations Conference on Trade and Development
UN-ECE	United Nations Economic Commission for Europe
UNEP	United Nations Environmental Program
UNESCO	United Nations Educational, Scientific and Cultural Organization
UNGA	United Nations General Assembly
UNIDO	United Nations Industrial Development Organization
UR	Uruguay Round URI Uruguay Round Implementation
VET	Vocational Education and Training
WAF	World Agriculture Forum
WCO	World Customs Organization
WG	Working Group
WGTP	Working Group on Trade Promotion
WIPO	World Intellectual Property Organization
WLN	Women Leaders' Network

WSSD	World Summit on Sustainable Development
WTO	World Tourism Organizations
WTOAGP	World Trade Organization Agreement on Government Procurement
WTTC	World Travel and Tourism Council
Y2K	Year 2000
YEAC	Young Entrepreneurs' Advisory Council
YEO	Young Entrepreneurs' Organisation

Chapter 2

ASIA PACIFIC ECONOMIC COOPERATION (APEC)[*]

Dick K. Nanto

INTRODUCTION

APEC is the leading organization in the Asia/Pacific that is working cooperatively to reduce trade and investment barriers among its 21 member economies, advance Asia-Pacific economic dynamism, and develop more of a sense of community among its members. U.S. participation in APEC is part of the broader U.S. debate over whether the United States should continue to pursue free trade and investment relations with Asia Pacific nations and whether and under what conditions the President should be provided fast-track trade negotiating (trade promotion) authority that might be used to negotiate free-trade agreements with APEC or with individual APEC members.

APEC also is of interest to Congress because 1) it is becoming a vehicle to generate trade initiatives to be considered by the World Trade Organization; 2) the APEC Leaders' Meeting provides an opportunity for the U.S. President to raise and discuss issues with the heads of other APEC countries; 3) any concrete trade or investment measures developed under APEC that require a change in existing U.S. law and cannot be done by presidential proclamation will need legislative

[*] Excerpted from CRS Report BTR-2059.

approval; and 4) in view of the debate over the North American Free-Trade Agreement (NAFTA), to create a free-trade arrangement that includes China, Japan, South Korea, Taiwan, Indonesia, Chile, and other Asian-Pacific nations is likely to be highly controversial.

BACKGROUND

On October 20-21, 2001, the Ninth APEC Leaders' Meeting (summit) was hosted by China in Shanghai. President Bush, Secretary of State Powell, U.S. Trade Representative Zoellick, Commerce Secretary Evans, and other members of the Administration attended. The official theme for APEC 2001 was "Meeting New Challenges in the New Century: Achieving Common Prosperity through Participation and Cooperation," with the sub-themes of (1) sharing the benefits of globalization and the new economy, (2) advancing trade and investment, and (3) promoting sustained economic growth. The war on terrorism and slowing world economic growth, however, dominated discussions.

The leaders' statement on counter-terrorism was the first time APEC dealt explicitly with a non-economic issue. APEC leaders also reaffirmed the goal of achieving free trade and investment among APEC members and to provide support for a new round of multilateral trade negotiations under the World Trade Organization. The leaders also issued the Shanghai Accord in which they committed themselves to broaden APEC's vision for the future by identifying a conceptual and policy framework to guide APEC in the new century. The Accord included clarifying APEC's roadmap for achieving the free trade and investment goals on schedule with an assessment of overall progress in 2005; promoting the adoption of appropriate trade policies for the New Economy; following up on the APEC Trade Facilitation Principles; pursuing greater transparency in economic governance; and strengthening APEC's implementation mechanism.

At the November 2000 APEC Leaders' Meeting held in Brunei, former President Clinton held bilateral summits with several leaders of APEC countries - including China, Japan, Russia, Singapore, and South Korea. Following the APEC meetings, Clinton traveled to Vietnam. As a part of the bilateral summits, the United States and Singapore announced that they would begin negotiations on a bilateral free trade agreement; the United States, New Zealand, Singapore, Brunei, and Chile agreed in principle to an "open skies" pact (eliminating restrictions on airline flights, prices, and routes among themselves), and the U.S. and China announced that China would ban certain missile-related exports in exchange for a lifting of U.S. sanctions prohibiting Chinese launches of American satellites.

APEC is an association of 21 economies bordering the Pacific Ocean who are working cooperatively to reduce barriers to trade and investment; ease the exchange of goods, services, resources, and technical know-how; and strengthen economic and technical cooperation. APEC began in 1989 as an Australian initiative in recognition of the growing interdependence among Asia-Pacific economies and in response to the free-trade areas which had developed in Europe and North America. Membership initially consisted of twelve countries but has now grown to twenty-one. They include the United States, Canada, Mexico, Peru, Chile, Japan, Russia, South Korea, China, Taiwan, Hong Kong, Indonesia, Brunei, Malaysia, Singapore, Thailand, Vietnam, the Philippines, Australia, New Zealand, and Papua New Guinea. The United States plays a key leadership role in APEC.

In 1994, in the Bogor Declaration, the leaders of APEC declared their intention to establish free trade and investment in the region by the year 2010 for industrialized members and 2020 for the others. This is being accomplished through concerted actions by individual APEC members, by pursuing trade and investment liberalization and trade facilitation in specific sectors, and by individual members establishing free-trade arrangements with each other.

LEGISLATION

Some trade liberalization under APEC arguably will require fast-track negotiating authority and congressional approval (H.R. 1446). U.S. financial support for APEC falls under the State Department's budget (H.R. 1646) under Contributions to International Organizations and has been $601,000 per year. Several bills would authorize negotiations to establish free-trade areas with APEC countries. These include S. 138 and S. 586 (with Chile) S. 935 (with Australia), S. 943 (with New Zealand), S. 944 (with the Republic of Korea), and H.R. 1566 (with Singapore, Australia, and New Zealand). H.Con.Res. 73 requests that during the APEC summit, the President call for the release of all Chinese political prisoners and Chinese ratification of the International Covenant on Civil and Political Rights. HCon.Res. 194 calls for APEC to allow participation by Taiwan's President Chen Shui-bian in the Shanghai Leader's Meeting.

Chapter 3

APEC AND FREE TRADE IN THE ASIA PACIFIC[†]

Dick K. Nanto

Asia Pacific Economic Cooperation (APEC) is an organization of eighteen economies surrounding the Pacific Ocean. Along with the World Trade Organization, it is the preeminent forum for promoting open trade and closer economic cooperation in the Asia/Pacific region. Its membership includes the United States, Canada, Mexico, and Chile in the Americas, Japan, South Korea, China, Taiwan, and Hong Kong in East Asia, the ASEAN nations of Indonesia, Brunei, Malaysia, Singapore, Thailand, and The Philippines, plus the Oceanic nations of Australia, New Zealand, and Papua New Guinea.

APEC is of interest to the Congress because it is committed to dismantling all barriers to trade and investment among its members by the year 2010 or 2020. This future free-trade area would cover nearly half the world's population, 60 percent of the world's gross domestic product, and 40 percent of world trade. APEC may define the framework for America's future trading relationships with the fast-growing Asian region. It also may provide trade and investment liberalization that goes beyond that available under the World Trade Organization. The APEC goal for liberalized trade and investment implies that free trade would

---

[†] Excerpted from CRS Report 96-1E. This expands, updates, and replaces Report No. 95-1079 E, *APEC and Free Trade in the Asia Pacific,* updated November 14, 1995.

be established with nations, such as Japan and China, with whom the United States runs large trade deficits and which account for many of the U.S. trade problems. (See figure 1.) Import barriers between economies such as China and Taiwan or South Korea and Japan that have diverted exports to the United States also would have to be eliminated. APEC's 1995 Action Agenda commits the United States to devising a U.S. Action Plan (to be presented in November 1996) that would lead to free trade with other APEC members by 2010 (with implementation beginning in 1997).

Figure 1. U.S. Merchandise Trade Balances with Selected Countries, 1994

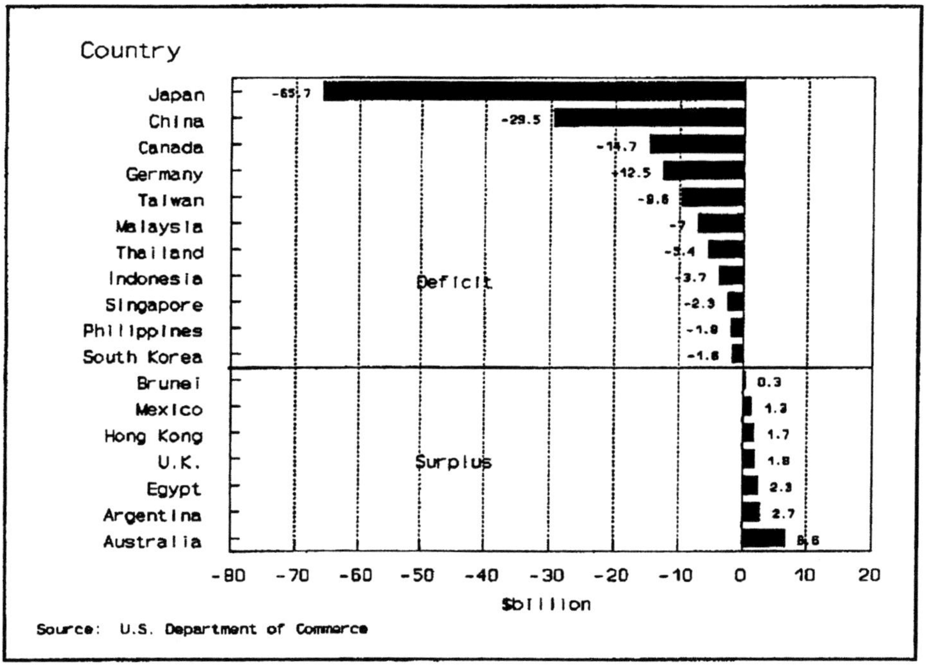

Source: U.S. Department of Commerce

The Clinton Administration has supported the APEC process and has viewed it as an institution that can bridge relationships with the Asia/Pacific in a manner similar to the post-war trans-Atlantic institutions bridged relationships with Europe. The Administration has stated that APEC is an important part of its Asia policy and represents a disciplined partnership for growth and opportunity that can create jobs, raise incomes, and give hope to people all across the Pacific.[1] In November 1995, however, Senate Republican Leader Bob Dole, called for a "cooling off period" while current trade pacts are assessed before embarking on new ones with Asia and Latin America. In discussing the Administration's request for new fast-track trade negotiating authority, Senator Dole asked why the Administration seemed to he in a hurry to pile on many more trade agreements as soon as possible from Latin America to Asia to Europe.[2]

Fast-track authority for considering new trade agreements has yet to he granted to the Clinton Administration to negotiate the APEC free-trade area. A question is whether, and at what point in the APEC process, fast-track authority would be necessary.

APEC was established in 1989 at the initiative of Australia. After six years, it is evolving from a "talk shop" into a force for trade liberalization. In 1993, the United States raised APEC's profile by inviting its leaders to attend a summit[3] in Seattle. This focused world attention on the fledgling organization. At its 1994 summit in Bogor, Indonesia, APEC leaders signed a declaration setting the goal of free and open trade and investment in APEC. The industrialized economies (United States, Japan, Canada, Australia, New Zealand, Singapore, and possibly others) are to achieve the goal by the year 2010 and the remaining economies to do so by 2020. The United States argued against allowing the additional 10 years for developing economies, but it was retained primarily at the insistence of China, South Korea, and Malaysia. The Bogor Declaration is a consensus, not legal, document.

The Asia/Pacific is one of the most vibrant economic areas in the world. U.S. trade with the Pacific has surpassed that with Europe. In 1960, East Asia accounted for only 4 percent of world gross domestic product (GDP). By 1991, it had reached 25 percent, and by the year 2000, it is expected to account for nearly one-third of world GDP.[4] Over the past decade, U.S. exports to Asian APEC members grew by 9.9 percent per year. Over the next six years, Asian APEC members are expected to invest $1.1 trillion in infrastructure projects. The opportunities for U.S. businesses in APEC are tremendous, but obstacles remain. According to the Clinton Administration, trade and investment liberalization

---

[1] The White House. Background Briefing by Senior Administration Officials, November 2, 1994. *and*, Remarks by the President Upon Arrival, Boeing Field, Seattle, Washington, November 18, 1993.

[2] Dole, Bob. Remarks in the Senate. *Congressional Record (Senate),* November 3, 1995. p. 16695-6.

[3] It is called a Leaders' Meeting because title heads of state of Taiwan and Hong Kong have not been able to attend because of objections from China.

[4] Perspectives. *Business America,* November 1994. pp. 4-5.

under APEC will help ensure that U.S. firms can take advantage of such opportunities there.[5]

THE OSAKA ACTION AGENDA

On November 19, 1996, the leaders of APEC met in Osaka, Japan, where they agreed to an Action Agenda that is intended to translate the Bogor Declaration into reality.[6] (Because of the U.S. Government shutdown, Vice President Al Gore attended in place of President Clinton.) The Osaka Action Agenda is the template for future APEC work to accomplish the three common goals of (1) trade and investment liberalization, (2) trade and investment facilitation, and (3) economic and technical cooperation. The Agenda laid out nine general principles for members to follow in devising a road map to reach APEC's free-trade goal. These general principles are to guide individual APEC members in devising national Action Plans (to be submitted in 1996) to attain the goal. The Action Plans are to be implemented starting in January 1997.

The general principles in the Action Plan included (1) comprehensiveness (all impediments are to be included), (2) WTO-consistency (consistent with the World Trade Organization), (3) comparability (equal sacrifice by all), (4) non-discrimination (benefits to be accorded to all APEC members and also to non-APEC countries on a reciprocal basis), (5) transparency, (6) standstill (no new barriers), (7) simultaneous start-continuous process-differentiated time tables (all start together in a continuous process to achieve long-term goal), (8) flexibility (a controversial principle that some argue allows for sensitive sectors, such as agriculture in Japan, China, and South Korea, to be liberalized more slowly), and (9) cooperation (to pursue economic and technical cooperation).

The Agenda also outlined actions that APEC economies were to take in fifteen specific areas. These included both actions by individual members and collectively by APEC in areas such as tariffs, non-tariff measures, services, investment, standards, customs procedures, intellectual property rights (IPRs), competition policy, and dispute mediation. Under IPRs, for example, the actions included ensuring that IPRs are granted expeditiously and that adequate and effective procedures and remedies are available against infringement of IPRs.

---

[5] U.S. Council of Economic Advisers. *Economic Report of the President.* Washington, U.S. Government Printing Office, 1995. p. 230-31.

[6] Asia Pacific Economic Cooperation. *The Osaka Action Agenda* (November 19, 1995). This and other APEC documents are available on the APEC 1995 Osaka Official Information site on the World Wide Web (http://apec.tokio.co.jp).

Under **dispute mediation,** the Action Plan called for more transparency of government laws, regulations, and administrative procedures with a view toward reducing and avoiding disputes regarding trade and investment matters. APEC hopes to promote dialogue and increased understanding, including exchange of views on any matter that may lead to a dispute, and cooperatively examine on a voluntary basis disputes that arise. It also is to examine possible future evolution of procedures for the resolution of disputes. The idea is that a voluntary mechanism would be established that would rely primarily on "Asian-style mediation" to address problems not covered by the WTO (such as antitrust policy) and which would provide a multilateral forum to resolve bilateral disputes.

Each APEC member also announced **initial actions** for liberalization and facilitation of trade and investment. (See appendix A.) These actions represented the first wide-ranging initiatives of APEC members to speed up implementing their Uruguay Round commitments. For the United States, the actions did not include any acceleration of tariff reductions. The United States merely indicated which of the Uruguay Round Agreements had been implemented and which were to be implemented in 1996. It also listed other liberalization and facilitation measures taken in 1995. Japan accelerated tariff reductions on 697 items by two years, reduced tariffs on 57 agricultural and fishery products, and announced numerous deregulatory measures.

The surprise package of initial actions came from China. China indicated that it would slash substantially the tariffs on over 4,000 items to bring its average tariff rate to less than 30 percent. It also eliminated import quotas and other import control measures on 170 items that account for about 30 percent of all such controls. This large package of measures was viewed by many as part of the attempt by China to meet the conditions for membership in the World Trade Organization.

Under **economic and technical cooperation,** the Action Agenda included compiling and sharing of data and information, surveys, training, seminars, research and technical demonstrations, and policy dialogues. Areas of cooperation included human resources development, industrial science and technology, small enterprises, energy, transportation, telecommunications, tourism, trade and investment data, trade promotion, marine resources conservation, fisheries, and agricultural technology.

Since Japan hosted the 1995 APEC meetings, it held the Chair and the responsibility to insure that the APEC process continued. Japan, however, took this opportunity to lead a group (including South Korea, China, and Taiwan) of members who argued for a weak definition of comprehensiveness[7] and insisted on including a general **principle of flexibility** that might allow them to placate certain sensitive sectors (particularly agriculture) by putting them on a slower timetable or possibly even exclude them from complete liberalization. This attempt by the Japan-led group to provide flexibility for sensitive sectors had been rebuffed by the other APEC senior officials in both the July and October 1995 meetings. The United States and twelve APEC members viewed the principle of comprehensiveness as vital to achieving the Bogor vision of free trade in APEC. In Osaka, APEC members reached a compromise that allowed the comprehensiveness principle to remain unchanged but added the principle of flexibility.[8] Japan reportedly hopes to interpret the flexibility principle to mean that it may postpone liberalizing its rice market until close to the year 2010. By then, many of its elderly rice farmers will have retired.

At Osaka, Malaysia also argued for making all APEC commitments "voluntary" (meaning that the free-trade target dates would not be binding). For the Bogor Declaration, Malaysia had attached its objections to establishing the goal of free trade and investment by the year 2010 or 2020. As a compromise, the word "voluntary" was added. The Osaka Leaders' Declaration stated APEC's resolve to "encourage...the evolving efforts **of voluntary liberalization** in the region," but the Osaka Action Agenda clearly declared under the comprehensiveness principle that "the APEC liberalization and facilitation process will be comprehensive, addressing all impediments to achieving the long-term goal of free and open trade and investment."[9] Japan's Trade Minister Ryutaro Hashimoto, who had argued for flexibility, stated clearly in a news conference announcing the declaration that the dates and commitments for free trade stood — voluntary or not.[10]

APEC members also disagreed over the **non-discrimination principle** or what has been termed "open regionalism." Japan has pressed for the benefits of APEC trade liberalization to be accorded even non-APEC trading partners on a most-favored-nation basis. Japan's Government has stated that it thought APEC

---

[7] October 25, 1995, Representatives Doug Bereuter and Howard L. Berman along with 27 other Members of the U.S. House of Representatives sent a letter to Secretary of State Warren Christopher and USTR Mickey Kantor urging the Administration not to weaken its resolve to press for "the promised comprehensive and detailed agenda for implementing the Bogor Declaration.[7]

[8] The flexibility principle reads: Considering the different levels of economic development among the APEC economies and the diverse circumstances in each economy, flexibility will be available in dealing with issues arising from such circumstances in the liberalization and facilitation process.

[9] APEC Osaka Action Agenda, p. 1.

[10] Tarrant, Bill. APEC Dodges Bullet, Keeps Free Trade Plan Momentum. Reuters News wire Service, November 17, 1995.

should not be a trading bloc that discriminates against outsiders. The problem with such unilateral trade liberalization, however, is that it invites free riders and makes generating public support difficult. The United States favored benefits to be accorded non-APEC countries on a reciprocal basis which has been the basis for other negotiations.[11] The APEC Declaration in Osaka emphasized its "resolute opposition to an inward-looking trading bloc" and committed itself to "firmly maintaining open regional cooperation." This arguably implies that benefits would be applied non-discriminately among APEC nations, but they would be extended to others only on a reciprocal basis. The Action Agenda stated that "the outcome of trade and investment liberalization...will be the actual reduction of barriers not only among APEC economies but also between APEC economies and non-APEC economies."[12]

China has been insisting that non-discrimination in APEC mean that it be ensured **most-favored-nation** (MFN) trading status by the United States. U.S. law, however, requires that China's MFN status be reviewed annually.[13] The compromise wording crafted for the Osaka Action Agenda was that "APEC members will apply or endeavor to apply the principle of non-discrimination between and among them in the process of liberalization and facilitation of trade and investment." According to U.S. Trade Representative Mickey Kantor, that bit of semantics was "just perfect" for the United States. China indicated that the wording was too vague to resolve the dispute.[14]

In terms of political feasibility, a key question remains to be answered. Would the public support a free trade area encompassing all major Asian and Pacific economies? In the United States, considering the acrimonious debate over implementing the North American Free Trade Agreement, how would the American people respond to a free-trade area that included China, Japan, and South Korea? Import-sensitive industries, such as textiles and apparel, also would likely oppose free imports from Asia.

APEC now is at a critical juncture. After six years of existence, many in the private sector are waiting for concrete measures that will facilitate trade rather than just having discussions and signing declarations. The Osaka meeting did result in enough clear action that APEC seems to have continued its momentum

---

[11] Johnstone, Christopher B. An Awkward Dance: The Osaka Summit, Japanese Leadership and the Future of APEC. *JEI Report,* October 20, 1995. p. 12.

[12] APEC Osaka Action Agenda, p. 1.

[13] U.S. Library of Congress. Congressional Research Service. *Most-Favored-Nation Status of the People's Republic of China.* CRS Issue Brief No. EB92094, December 4, 1995 (updated regularly). Washington, 1995. 9p.

[14] Sieg, Linda. U.S. Trade Envoy Says APEC Has Reached "Good" Deal. Reuters News Service. November 16, 1995.

and maintained its credibility and support from business communities throughout the Pacific rim.

APEC'S EVOLUTION AND ACTIVITIES

APEC began in 1989 as an Australian initiative in response to free-trade areas which had developed in Europe and North America. Originally intended to exclude the United States and Canada, APEC was to provide an institution and forum for consultation and coordination on economic issues of importance to East Asia and Australia/New Zealand. Ultimately, however, membership was expanded to encompass North America.

Membership in APEC initially included twelve countries but has now grown to eighteen. The founding members were the United States, Canada, Japan, South Korea, ASEAN (Brunei, Indonesia, Malaysia, Philippines, Singapore, and Thailand, but not Vietnam), Australia, and New Zealand. In 1991, the People's Republic of China, Taiwan, and Hong Kong joined. In 1993, Mexico and Papua New Guinea were admitted, as was Chile in 1994. Additional membership decisions have been deferred until 1996 when applications from Vietnam, Russia, India, Mongolia, Panama, and other countries may be considered.

APEC symbolizes post-Cold War relationships in which trade and investment have become an important pillar in the foundation underlying world peace and security. While trade still may be used as a punitive measure in U.S. foreign policy, it also may become a catalyst for change in countries with authoritarian governments or isolated markets. APEC promotes cooperation and trade among the nations of the Pacific Basin, encourages open trading systems rather than trading blocs, keeps the United States engaged in the region, and provides the Asia Pacific with a counterweight to the European Union. In 1993, support by APEC for concluding the Uruguay Round GATT negotiations placed pressure on Europe that hastened the signing of the final agreement.

APEC is a far cry from either the European Union or North American Free Trade Agreement (NAFTA) — or even AFTA, the ASEAN Free Trade Area. APEC's goal of free trade is to be phased in over the next quarter century. Only the framework now exists to lead APEC members toward that goal. APEC is not a negotiating body nor are its decisions legally binding on its members. APEC's staff is modest, and its consensus-based decision-making is cumbersome. Rather than a trade bloc, it may serve as a building block toward greater trade liberalization and cooperation world wide.

In terms of APEC activities, the annual **Leaders Meeting** is attended by heads of state except for those from Taiwan and Hong Kong (because of China's objections). Although APEC confines its agenda to economic issues, the heads of state at bilateral meetings conducted before and after the "summit" have discussed concerns over international security, human rights, and other issues.

The 1996 Leaders Meeting is to be held in The Philippines, the 1997 meeting in Thailand, and the 1998 meeting in Malaysia.[15]

The annual **Joint Ministerial Meeting** preceding the Leaders Meeting is attended by foreign, trade, and some commerce ministers from member states. The chair of both the Ministerial and Leaders' Meetings is held by the host country. Management of substance is handled under ministerial direction through Senior Officials Meetings. Specialized APEC ministerial meetings also are held. In 1993, APEC created a secretariat in Singapore with an Executive Director, 40-person staff, and a modest budget ($2.8 million in 1996). In 1995, Japan indicated that it would provide APEC with 10 billion yen (about $100 million) to fund APEC cooperative projects.[16]

Most of the specific tasks facing APEC are being addressed in committees or working groups that deal with economic issues of importance to the region. These include the Committee on Trade and Investment, the Economic Committee, and the following working groups: (1) Trade and Investment Data, (2) Trade Promotion, (3) Industrial Science and Technology, (4) Human Resources Development, (5) Energy Cooperation, (6) Marine Resource Conservation, (7) Telecommunications, (8) Transportation, (9) Tourism, and (10) Fisheries. The groups develop activities aimed at expanding economic cooperation among members. Each working group has one or more shepherds (members) who take responsibility for coordinating the work of the group.

In 1992, APEC formed the Eminent Persons Group (EPG) and charged it with developing a "vision" for APEC's future. In 1994, the EPG recommended that APEC establish the goal of free trade, and, in 1995, recommended ways to achieve that vision. The EPG completed its task in 1995. In 1994, APEC also formed the Pacific Business Forum to provide a channel for private sector interests to be expressed.[17] In 1995, APEC set up another business group to advise APEX) called the Asian Business Advisory Council.

---

15 In December 1995, the Flag Desecration Constitutional Amendment was held up in the Senate because of a threatened filibuster because the Senate had not acted on the appointments of several ambassadors, including the U.S. Ambassador to APEG.

16 Japan to Offer 10 Billion Yen for APEC Trade Liberalization. DowJones Newswire Service, November 14, 1995.

17 [U.S. Department of State]. *APEC 1995, A for the Perplexed.* Washington, 1995. 18P. See: Eminent Persons Group. *Achieving the APEC Vision, Free and Open Trade in the Asia Pacific.*

Heretofore, all APEC declarations have been nonbinding and generally lacking in specific measures to be taken. As the countries submit their Action Plans that are to lead to free trade and investment, however, member nations may have to seek approval for their actions through their legislative processes. For the United States, this would normally require consideration under fast-track authority for approval of trade agreements.

In 1995, U.S. Defense Secretary William Perry started a debate about whether APEC should be expanded to include consideration of regional security issues. Heretofore, all such discussions were confined to bilateral summit meetings surrounding the Leaders Meetings. APEC has carefully kept its distance from security matters for fear that such issues would cause divisions within the group — particularly between China and other members, such as Taiwan, the United States, and Japan. Such divisions could thwart cooperation in achieving economic goals. The consensus in 1995, seemed to be that regional security issues should be discussed in the ASEAN Regional Forum rather than in APEC.[18] The ASEAN Regional Forum usually meets after the ASEAN Ministerial Conference and, in addition to the seven members of ASEAN, includes the United States, China, Russia, Japan, South Korea, Australia, New Zealand, Canada, and the European Union. It provides the largest pan-Pacific forum for discussing security issues.[19]

THE APEC REGION AND TRADE

The Asia Pacific region contains nearly half the world's population, 60 percent of the world's gross domestic product, and 40 percent of its trade. U.S. trade with APEC nations, even excluding Canada and Mexico, is twice as great as that with the European Union. In the near term, Asian markets (except for Japan's) are expected to grow more rapidly than those in North America or Europe. Since the U.S. market already is relatively open, Americans stand to gain more from the lowering of trade barriers abroad than other countries have in further reductions in such barriers in the United States. Import duties on automobiles in Southeast Asia,

---

Singapore, APEC Secretariat, 1994. 80 p. ___. *Implementing the APEC Vision.* Singapore, APEC Secretariat, 1995. Pacific Business Forum. *The Osaka Action Plan: Roadmap to Realising the APEC Vision.* Asia-Pacific Economic Cooperation, 1995. 57p.

18 Moosa, Eugene. Regional Security Remains a Taboo at APEC. Reuters Newswire Service. November 19, 1995.

19 U.S. Library of Congress. Congressional Research Service. *Regional Security Consultative Organizations in East Asia and Their Implications for the United States.* CRS Report No. 94-79, by Larry Niksch. Washington, 1994. 15p.

for example, range from 30 to 60 percent compared with 2.5 percent in the United States.

U.S. trade with most of these Asian countries, however, is highly unbalanced. In 1994, of the $151 billion U.S. deficit in merchandise trade with the world, $130 billion or 86 percent was with APEC Asia. In short, in as much as the U.S. trade deficit is a problem, that problem largely centers around the Asian APEC member countries. (See table 1.)

Table 1. U.S. Merchandise Trade with APEC Nations/Groups, 1994 ($ million)

Nation/Group	U.S. Exports	U.S. Imports	Balance	Trade Deficit as % of Total U.S. Trade Deficit
Japan	53,481	119,149	-65,668	43.4%
South Korea	18,028	19,658	-1,630	1.1%
China/Hong Kong	20,732	48,479	-27,747	18.3%
Taiwan	17,078	26,711	-9,633	6.4%
Total Chinese Economic Area	37,810	75,190	-37,380	24.7%
Total NE Asia	109,319	213,997	-104,678	69.1%
Brunei	376	46	330	-0.2%
Indonesia	2,811	6,523	-3,712	2.5%
Malaysia	6,965	13,977	-7,012	4.6%
Singapore	13,022	15,360	-2,338	1.5%
Thailand	4,861	10,307	-5,446	3.6%
Philippines	3,888	5,720	-1,832	1.2%
Vietnam	172	50	122	-0.1%
Total ASEAN	32,095	51,983	-19,888	13.1%
Total NE Asia/ASEAN	141,414	265,980	-124,566	82.3%
Australia	9,781	3,200	6,581	-4.3%
New Zealand	1,508	1,421	87	-0.1%
Chile	2,776	1,822	954	-0.6%
Papua New Guinea	65	108	-43	0.0%
Total APEC	320,467	450,921	-130,454	86.2%
Total NAFTA	165,095	178,440	-13,345	8.8%
Total World	512,416	663,830	-151,414	100.0%

Note: N.A. = not applicable. NAFTA includes the United States, Canada, and Mexico
Source: Data are from U.S. Department of Commerce

Despite the great amount of trade and economic growth in the Asia Pacific region, only four trading arrangements currently exist among APEC countries. The North American Free Trade Agreement, the agreement for Closer Economic Relations between Australia and New Zealand, the ASEAN Free Trade Area (that reduces but does not eliminate trade barriers within ASEAN by the year 2003), and the Chile-Mexican Free Trade Agreement. The United States, however, has agreed to complete negotiations to create a Free Trade Area of the Americas by the year 2005. Negotiations for Chile to join NAFFA also began in 1995.[20] In response to APEC, the European Union has floated the idea of a trans-Atlantic free-trade agreement. In 1995, this was considered but dropped. On December 3, 1995, however, the United States and the European Union announced a New Transatlantic Agenda which includes a goal of creating a New Transatlantic Marketplace aimed at reducing barriers to trade.[21]

Japan and its neighboring Asian economies, however, are building trade and investment networks that could develop into a powerful trading bloc, if organized. Japanese and Chinese production networks have been proliferating in East and Southeast Asia. Japan also has been increasing the percentage of its trade that is conducted in yen, although a yen bloc still seems quite distant. Trade friction, moreover, has induced many of the Asian nations to diversify their exports away from the U.S. market and toward each other.

A key difference between APEC and the European Union or NAFTA is the degree of diversity among member states. APEC members range from locations encompassing the Gobi Desert in the north to Cape Horn in the south with populations ranging from the 1.2 billion people in China to the 268,000 in Brunei, and spanning the economic development spectrum from the industrial giants of the United States and Japan to the newly industrialized economies such as South Korea and Singapore on to poor nations such as Papua New Guinea. Cultures range from European to Asian and to Latin American. Religions, types of governments, economic systems, and average educational levels, likewise, differ greatly.

EAST ASIAN ECONOMIC CAUCUS

The momentum in APEC along with Japan's reluctance to risk offending the United States has sidelined a proposal by Malaysian Prime Minister Mahathir to form an East Asian Economic Caucus, a consultative caucus within APEC. Membership would include only Asia members of APEC and would provide a forum for Asian nations to coordinate policies and provide Japan with Asian points of view before multilateral meetings, such as the G-7. The Bush

[20] U.S. Library of Congress. Congressional Research Service. *Trade and the America.* CRS Issue Brief No. 1695017, November 29, 1995 (updated regularly). Washington, 1995. 16p.

[21] U.S. Department of State. The New Transatlantic Agenda, Pact Sheet. November 30, 1995.

Administration opposed the creation of the EAEC directly, while the Clinton Administration has been highly skeptical of it. Without Japan's participation, the EAEC is not likely to be organized.

In order to circumvent U.S. objections, in December 1996, ASEAN plans an informal summit with itself and the countries invited to join the EAEC, The idea is for ASEAN leaders to meet with other East Asian heads of state to discuss issues. ASEAN claims such a caucus would be no different from other caucuses which exist elsewhere in the world.[22] Whether or not other East Asian leaders will attend and whether this will be viewed as the launch of an EAEC-type of organization is yet to be seen.

APPENDIX A: SUMMARY OF OSAKA INITIAL ACTIONS

The following is a summary of initial add-ons announced by APEC members in Osaka on November 19, 1995, for liberalization and facilitation of trade and investment. These actions represent the first wide-ranging initiatives by APEC members to use the organization to accelerate the implementation of their Uruguay Round commitments, to deepen and broaden the outcomes of the Uruguay Round, and to launch deregulation measures.

AUSTRALIA: To open its telecommunications sector to competition from July 1, 1997. Advancing tariff cuts offered in Uruguay Round of global trade talks so that final bound rates for industrial products will be achieved in 1998 and on agricultural products in 1999.

BRUNEI: Submitted previously announced proposals to reduce tariffs on 688 items. To amend trademarks and copyright laws.

CANADA: Submitted previously announced measures to reduce 1,500 tariff lines and extended NAFTA preferential investment provisions to all investors.

CHILE: Bringing forward implementation of tariff commitments across the board and eliminating trade distortive agricultural support measures.

CHINA: From 1996, to slash overall tariffs by an average of 30 percent on more than 4,000 tariff lines. Pledged to eliminate quota, licensing and other import control measures on about 170 tariff lines accounting for more than 30 percent of the commodities now subject to such quotas and licensing requirements. Designated Shanghai and other cities as pilot bases for Sino-foreign joint ventures.

[22] ASEAN Plans 'Virtual' EAEC Meeting At 'Informal' Summit Next Year. *The Daily Japan Digest*, December 14, 1995. p. 1-2.

HONG KONG: To place an additional five percent of its imports in the duty-free category; to decontrol telecom and financial sectors.

INDONESIA: Submitted previously announced reductions on 96 percent of all tariffs exceeding 5 percent and is accelerating the elimination of non-tariff barriers faster than required under the Uruguay Round accord.

JAPAN: Bringing forward tariff cuts on 697 industrial and mining products. Announced 50 deregulatory measures, including easing visa restrictions for business executives.

SOUTH KOREA: After liberalizing 53 additional businesses for foreign investments in 1995, is liberalizing 89 more in 1996, 38 more in 1997, and 21 more by 2000. As announced previously, will lower tariffs on automobiles and other items while deregulating railways, food inspections, and customs procedures.

MALAYSIA: As previously announced, accelerated cuts in tariffs on 2,317 items in 1995 and 1,047 items in 1996, liberalizing financial services, capital markets, telecommunications, electricity and shipping.

MEXICO: Submitted previously announced proposals liberalizing foreign investment in railroads, satellite communications, natural gas distribution, transportation and financial services.

NEW ZEALAND: Unilaterally reducing tariffs so about half will be zero with the rest no higher than 15 percent by 2000. To implement agreement in intellectual property rights ahead of schedule.

PAPUA NEW GUINEA: Negotiating to join the World Trade Organisation. Will cut tariffs and dismantle non-tariff barriers.

PHILIPPINES: Will lower all tariffs to 5 percent by 2004 and ease regulations on foreign investment under previously announced measures.

SINGAPORE: Will accelerate Uruguay Round tariff reductions. Will implement agreements on intellectual property and investment measures ahead of schedule; to deregulate state-run employee pension fund, telecommunications, and electricity sectors.

TAIWAN: Cutting tariffs on 758 items, relaxing bans and quotas on some imported goods and opening more sectors to foreign investment.

THAILAND: Accelerated cuts on 25 percent of the tariff items in its Uruguay Round commitments. Opening up its financial services sector and setting up an intellectual property and trade court.

UNITED STATES: Relaxing customs procedures and export controls and streamlining government procurement practices under previously announced measures.

Chapter 4

APEC: ENERGY ISSUES AND TRENDS[‡]

Lowell Feld

PREFACE

Asia-Pacific Economic Cooperation (APEC) member economies are beginning to prepare their energy sectors to meet the internal and external challenges of the 21st century. In response to this effort, the U.S. Department of Energy, in conjunction with the city of San Diego, is hosting the APEC Energy Ministers' Conference in May 2000. The theme for the APEC Energy Ministers' Conference, "Turning Vision Into Reality," refers to the implementation of policies to foster the creation of the energy infrastructure to meet the economic and environmental needs of the 21st century. APEC member economies will focus on strategies to implement existing policy commitments and to enhance investment in clean and sustainable energy development, on opportunities for regional energy market integration, and on continued transition to a market-oriented business climate. The regions' energy ministers and representatives of the private sector, multilateral institutions, and nongovernment organizations will work together to create a vision for the 21st century that will support clean and sustainable energy and economic development.

[‡] Excerpted from the Department of Energy website: http://www.eia.doe.gov.

ENERGY ECONOMY PROFILES

- As a group, the Asia-Pacific Economic Cooperation (APEC) economies account for over half of world energy production and consumption. In 1998, APEC consumed 220 quadrillion Btu (quads) of energy and produced 203 quads, making it a net energy importer of 17 quads.
- In 1998, APEC accounted for 65%-70% of world natural gas, coal, and "other" production and consumption. APEC also accounted for around 56% of nuclear power production and consumption, and 48% of hydroelectric. APEC accounted for around 35% of world oil output and consumed 36%.
- In 1998, APEC was a significant (around 30 quads, or 14 million barrels per day — bbl/d) net oil importer. The United States was by far the largest net oil importer in APEC, followed by Japan, South Korea, Chinese Taipei, China, Singapore, and Thailand. All other APEC members were very small net importers or exporters, with the exceptions of Russia, Mexico, Canada, and Indonesia, all significant net oil exporters.
- APEC was a significant net natural gas exporter in 1998, largely as a result of Russian gas exports to Europe. Canada exported large volumes of gas, almost exclusively within APEC (to the United States). Japan imported large volumes of natural gas in 1998, all in the form of liquefied natural gas (LNG), mainly from Southeast Asia.
- APEC also was a significant net coal exporter in 1998, mainly coming from Australia, the United States, Indonesia, and China (Japan and South Korea were large net coal importers).
- Between 1980 and 1998, oil was consistently the leading fuel consumed within APEC, followed by coal, natural gas, hydroelectricity, nuclear power, and "other".
- As far as APEC energy production is concerned, since 1980 coal has surpassed natural gas and oil in first place, while natural gas has surpassed oil for second place. Nuclear and hydroelectricity for years have been approximately tied for fourth place, while "other" consistently has ranked last over the time period.

APEC: Energy Production and Consumption by Fuel, 1998

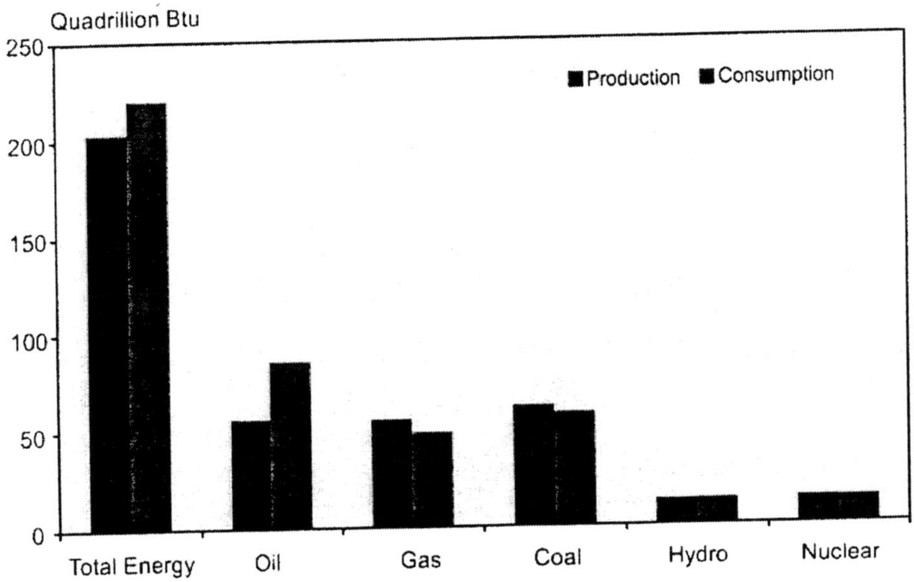

- From 1980 through 1998, APEC energy consumption increased 35%. Oil consumption increased by 16% over that period, natural gas by 37%, hydroelectricity by 38%, coal by 48%, nuclear by 198%, and "other" (wind, geothermal, etc.) by 577% (from an extremely low base).
- From 1980 through 1998, APEC energy production increased 78%. Oil production increased by 40% over that period and natural gas by 113%. Hydroelectric output rose 64%, coal 75%, nuclear 233%, and "other" 574% (from an extremely low base).

APEC: Energy Consumption by Fuel Type, 1980-1998

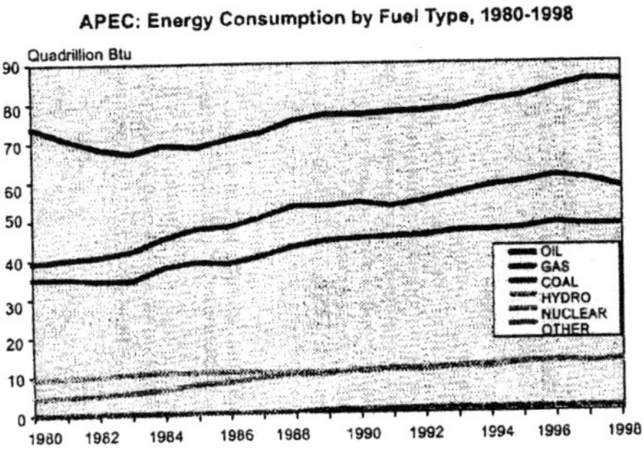

APEC: Energy Production by Fuel Type, 1980-1998

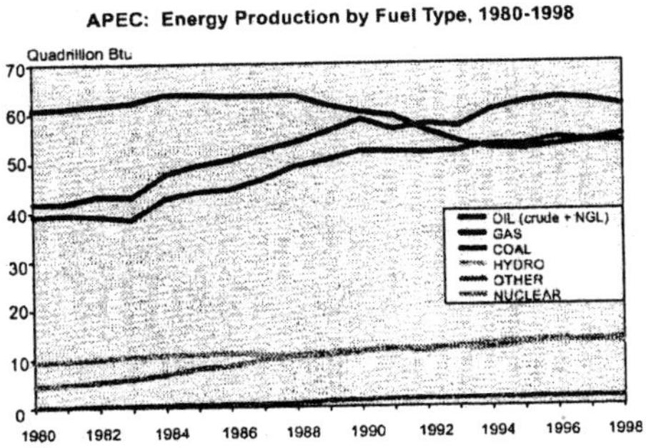

DATA TABLES FOR APEC MEMBER ECONOMIES

APEC Economic and Demographic Indicators

	Gross Domestic Product* (GDP)			Per Capita GDP, 1999E (U.S. Dollars)	Population, 1998E (Millions)
	1999E (Billions of U.S. Dollars)	Real GDP Growth Rate			
		1999 Estimate	2000 Projection		
Australia	$393.9	3.9%	3.5%	$20,734	18.8
Brunei	NA	NA	NA	NA	0.3
Canada	$631.9	3.5%	2.6%	$20,695	30.3
Chile	$69.8	-0.5%	6.2%	$4,643	14.8
China (PRC)	$1,026.9	7.3%	6.9%	$809	1,255.7
Hong Kong, China	$161.5	1.2%	3.0%	$23,538	6.7
Indonesia	$148.3	-1.1%	3.2%	$715	204.4
Japan	$4,366.3	1.3%	2.0%	$34,482	126.4
Malaysia	$79.3	4.9%	5.8%	$3,503	21.4
Mexico	$469.8	3.5%	4.8%	$4,905	100.2
New Zealand	$53.0	3.0%	4.2%	$13,850	3.8
Papua New Guinea	$4.1	1.4%	1.4%	$890	4.3
Peru	$57.1	3.0%	6.5%	$2.269	24.8
Philippines	$79.0	3.2%	4.7%	$1,031	75.2
Russia	$149.7	1.5%	2.0%	$1,024	146.5
Singapore	$87.8	4.9%	5.9%	$27,293	3.9
South Korea	$424.6	9.0%	5.9%	$9,062	46.4
Chinese Taipei	$292.8	5.3%	6.7%	$13,296	21.8
Thailand	$129.6	3.7%	4.2%	$2,083	61.2
United States	$9,233.3	3.9%	3.1%	$33,918	270.3
Vietnam	$34.2	4.0%	4.5%	$417	77.6
Total*	$17,893	3.5%	3.3%	$7,051	2,514.8

*GDP total excludes Brunei. All GDP figures use market exchange rates.
E=Estimate
Source: WEFA Outlooks 1Q2000

APEC Energy Consumption and Carbon Dioxide Emissions, 1998

	Energy Consumption							Carbon Dioxide Emissions [2] (Million metric tons of carbon)
	Total (Quadrillion Btu)	Petroleum	Natural Gas	Coal	Nuclear	Hydroelectric	Other [1]	
Australia	4.3	38%	19%	38%	0%	4%	1%	83
Brunei	0.1	51%	49%	0%	0%	0%	0%	1
Canada	11.8	31%	26%	10%	6%	29%	-2%	138
Chile	0.9	55%	13%	15%	0%	17%	0.2%	14
China (PRC)	33.9	25%	3%	66%	0.4%	6%	-0.2%	740
Hong Kong, China	0.8	57%	12%	31%	0%	0%	11%	13
Indonesia	3.6	56%	29%	12%	0%	2%	1%	68
Japan	21.3	53%	13%	14%	15%	4%	1%	288
Malaysia	1.7	52%	42%	4%	0%	2%	(s)	28
Mexico	5.9	65%	23%	4%	1%	4%	2%	95
New Zealand	0.8	34%	23%	6%	0%	31%	6%	9
Papua New Guinea	0.04	78%	9%	0.1%	0%	13%	0%	1
Peru	0.5	67%	3%	3%	0%	27%	0.3%	7
Phillippines	1.1	71%	(s)	10%	0%	4%	15%	18
Russia	26.0	20%	54%	16%	4%	6%	-1%	405
Singapore	1.3	96%	4%	(s)	0%	0%	0%	26
South Korea	6.9	60%	8%	19%	12%	1%	(s)	108
Chinese Taipei	3.3	50%	6%	30%	10%	3%	0%	59
Thailand	2.3	61%	24%	12%	0%	3%	0.2%	43
United States	94.8	39%	23%	23%	8%	4%	4%	1,495
Vietnam	0.7	50%	3%	22%	0%	25%	0%	12
Total	222.2	38%	22%	26%	6%	6%	2%	3,652

[1] For all countries, "other" includes biomass, geothermal, solar, and wind electric power. For the United States, "other" also includes biomass, geothermal, and solar energy not used for electric power generation, imports of geothermal electric power from Mexico, and net imports of electric power derived from nonrenewable sources. For all other countries, "other" includes net imports of electricity. A negative value for "other" indicates that the country was a net exporter of electricity.

[2] Includes carbon dioxide emissions from the consumption of petroleum, natural gas, and coal, and from the flaring of natural gas. Tons of carbon can be converted to tons of carbon dioxide gas by multiplying by 3.667.

(S)=Value less than 0.05%

Note: Percentages may not add to 100% because of independent rounding.

Source: Energy Information Administration, International Energy Database, April 14, 2000.

APEC Energy Supply Indicators Table

	Fossil Fuel Proved Reserves			Fossil Fuel Production, 1998			Electric Generating Capacity, 1/1/98 (Million kilowatts)	Crude Oil Refining Capacity, 1/1/00 (Thousand barrels per day)
	Crude Oil, 1/1/00 (Million barrels)	Natural Gas, 1/1/00 (Trillion cubic feet)	Coal, 12/31/97 (Billion short tons)	Petroleum [1] (Million barrels per day)	Dry Natural Gas (Trillion cubic feet)	Coal (Million short tons)		
Australia	2,895	44.6	99.6	0.6	1.1	314	39	812
Brunei	1,350	13.8	0	0.2	0.3	0	0.4	9
Canada	4,931	63.9	9.5	2.7	6.0	83	112	1,912
Chile	150	3.5	1.3	0.02	0.1	1	8	205
China (PRC)	24,000	48.3	126.2	3.2	0.8	1,351	254	4,347
Hong Kong, China	0	0	0	0	0	0	11	0
Indonesia	4,980	72.3	5.8	1.6	2.2	66	20	993
Japan	59	1.4	0.9	0.1	0.1	4	219	4,998
Malaysia	3,900	81.7	0	0.8	1.4	0.2	14	524
Mexico	28,399	30.1	1.3	3.5	1.3	11	38	1,525
New Zealand	127	2.5	0.6	0.1	0.2	4	8	98
Papua New Guinea	333	5.4	0	0.1	0	0	0.5	0
Peru	355	9.0	1.2	0.1	0.0	0.0	5	182
Philippines	289	2.8	0.3	0	0	1	12	401
Russia	48,573	1,700.0	173.1	6.1	20.9	272	206	6,673
Singapore	0	0	0	0	0	0	6	1,255
South Korea	0	0	0.1	0.1	0	5	44	2,540
Chinese Taipei	4	2.7	0	0	0	0.1	26	770
Thailand	296	12.5	2.2	0.1	0.6	22	17	713
United States	21,034	164.0	275.1	9.3	18.9	1,119	779	16,541
Vietnam	600	6.8	0.2	0.2	0	12	5	0.8
Total	142,274	2,265	697.4	28.8	53.9	3,266	1,822	44,498

[1]Includes crude oil, natural gas plant liquids, other liquids, and refinery processing gain. Sources: Crude Oil and Natural Gas Reserves: PennWell Publishing Co., Oil Gas Journal, 12/20/99. Crude Oil Refining Capacity: PennWell Publishing Co., Oil Gas Journal, 12/20/99. All Other Data: Energy Information Administration, International Energy Database, April 2000.

ENVIRONMENTAL ISSUES

Climate Change and Carbon Emissions

- APEC includes six of the world's ten largest carbon emitters (using 1998 data): the **United States** at 1,495 million metric tons; **China** at 740 million metric tons; **Russia** at 405 million metric tons; **Japan** at 288 million metric tons; **Canada** at 139 million metric tons; and **South Korea** at 108 million metric tons.

- The **United States** has signed (but not ratified) the Kyoto Protocol, under which it has pledged to reduce its carbon emissions 7% below 1990 levels by 2008-2012. U.S. carbon emissions have continued to rise steadily since 1990 and are predicted to reach almost 2,000 million metric tons per year by 2020.

- **China**, the world's most populous nation, is heavily reliant on highly carbon-intensive coal. As a non-Annex I developing country, China has no Kyoto Protocol obligation to reduce emissions and is expected to surpass the United States to become the world's largest carbon emitter by 2020. The amounts of energy and carbon consumed per dollar of GDP have decreased dramatically in China over the past two decades, while GDP growth rates have averaged around 10%.

Smoke Stack

- **Russia's** carbon emissions have dropped from 583 million metric tons of carbon in 1992 to 405 million metric tons in 1998. This situation is explained more by Russia's deteriorating economic situation during the 1990s than by more energy-efficient consumption.

- Under the Kyoto Protocol, **Japan** committed to reduce its carbon emissions 6% below 1990 levels by 2008-2012. While its carbon emissions began to decline in 1997, they remain above 1990 levels. Japan's Ministry of Trade and Industry is revising its long-term energy plan to reduce energy consumption and carbon emissions. Japan is one of the least energy- and carbon-intensive economies in the world.
- **Canada** made a Kyoto Protocol commitment to reduce its carbon emissions 6% below 1990 levels by 2008-2012. While Canada has not yet ratified the treaty, the government has approved (in principle) an expenditure of $1.63 billion over five years for a package of greenhouse gas emissions control and mitigation measures, including: improving mass transit, establishing tax incentives for the purchase of energy efficient technologies, bolstering an international emissions trading program, and improving Canada's domestic climate research.
- **South Korea's** energy use and carbon emissions increased dramatically throughout the 1980s and 1990s (until the 1997 Asian financial crisis), catapulting South Korea into the top ten world carbon emitters.
- APEC members **Singapore** and **Papua New Guinea** are members of the Alliance of Small Island States, representing countries that are most at risk of suffering adverse effects (including loss of territory to rising sea levels) due to climate change.

Non-thermal Energy

- The volcanically active "Ring of Fire" in the Pacific Ocean affords many APEC members significant geothermal energy potential. Only about 17 countries in the world produced geothermal energy in 1998, and six of the world's top ten producers are APEC members: the **United States** at 13.9 bkwh, the **Philippines** at 7.6 bkwh, **Mexico** at 5.4 bkwh, **Japan** at 3.5 bkwh, **Indonesia** at 2.5 bkwh, and **New Zealand** at 2.0 bkwh.
- Half of the world's top ten hydroelectricity producers in 1998 were APEC members: **Canada** at 329.3 bkwh, the **United States** at 324.1

bkwh, **China** at 202.9 bkwh, **Russia** at 150.5 bkwh, and **Japan** at 89.5 bkwh.

- While hydropower does not produce greenhouse gases, it is not without environmental costs. Some major hydroelectric dam construction projects in APEC have been controversial: the 18.2-GW Three Gorges dam in **China**, slated for completion in 2009, could have serious environmental repercussions; construction of the 570-MW Ralco dam on the Bio-bio River in **Chile** was suspended in February 2000, in part due to environmental concerns and in part to concerns over the displacement of indigenous peoples (construction likely will resume in the spring of 2000).
- Five of the world's ten largest nuclear electricity producers are APEC members: in 1998, the **United States** produced 674 bkwh of nuclear electricity, **Japan** 318 bkwh, **Russia** 98 bkwh, **South Korea** 82 bkwh, and **Canada** 68 bkwh.

Windmill

- Although nuclear power does not emit greenhouse gases, nuclear waste disposal and the possibility of nuclear accidents pose potential environmental threats. All of the major APEC nuclear power producers face the controversial issue of how best to store radioactive nuclear waste. While some countries' nuclear reactors are more prone to accidents than others, all must deal with the possibility of accidents resulting in radioactive contamination and negative public opinion associated with smaller accidents.

Air Pollution

- A report released in 1998 by the World Health Organization (WHO) noted that seven of the ten most polluted cities in the world are in **China**. Sulfur dioxide and soot caused by coal combustion are two major air pollutants, resulting in the formation of acid rain, which now falls on about 30% of China's total land area.
- Mexico City, **Mexico**, is among the world's most polluted cities. Exhaust fumes from Mexico City's 2.5 million cars are the main source of air pollutants, and the city's location in a basin exacerbates the problem, as pollutants are trapped above the city.

Smog in the City

- **Chile's** capital city, Santiago, suffers extreme air pollution, although its air quality has improved in the 1990s. Santiago's location in an Andes Mountain valley traps emissions from the city's large and quickly growing fleet of privately owned vehicles. Santiago's air usually is considered to be the most polluted of any South American city and is among the most polluted in the world, especially in terms of suspended particulates.

Traffic Smog

- There are over three million motor vehicles in Jakarta, **Indonesia**. Jakarta's Land Transport Organization estimates that 70% of Jakarta's air has been contaminated by chemical compounds from vehicle emissions, which are associated with a variety of health concerns. The government began to take steps to phase out the use of leaded gasoline in 1999, but complete elimination of leaded gasoline is not expected until 2004.

- The **United States** Environmental Protection Agency in March 2000 released a legislative framework to replace MTBE, an additive in gasoline that reduces gasoline's contribution to ground level ozone, with renewable additives such as ethanol. The Clean Air Act of 1990 required areas with severe ozone smog problems to use reformulated gasoline; 87% of reformulated gasoline uses MTBE, which is associated with ground water pollution.

ELECTRICITY

- Electricity demand grew rapidly in the APEC economies during most of the 1990s, as a result of overall economic growth. With many APEC economies currently recovering from the effects of the financial crisis of 1997-1998, a short-term pause in this power growth is being reversed. The developing economies of Asia are projected to have the strongest growth in the world in electricity demand over the next 20 years.
- **China** is emerging from a short-term oversupply problem in its electricity sector. While residential demand continued to grow from 1997 to 1998, industrial demand was flat. The Chinese authorities responded to the oversupply by closing some older small thermal plants and announcing a temporary moratorium on new power project approvals. Even so, there was 70 MW worth of new capacity under construction at the beginning of 1999. The largest project is the Three Gorges Dam, which when completed (possibly in 2009) will have 26 separate 700 MW generators, for a total of 18.2 GW.
- **China** plans eventually to create a unified national power grid, in place of today's patchwork of regional grids, and to develop a modern competitive market for electric power.
- **China's** electric power demand is projected to grow by 5.7% annually through 2020, which will necessitate a massive flow of investment in new generating capacity, if it is to keep up with demand.
- **Japan's** electric power sector is expected to show modest growth rates over the next two decades. While thermal power plants generated 57% of Japan's electricity in 1998, Japan is expected to shift toward more nuclear power, which currently makes up about one- third of Japan's electricity supply.

- **Japan** undertook a partial deregulation of its electric power sector in March 2000. Under the new scheme, large industrial power consumers, which account for about 30% of total power consumption, will be able to purchase their power in a competitive market.
- **Indonesia** is in the process of dealing with the financial problems in its electric power sector caused by lower-than-expected demand, which stemmed partially from the effects of the Asian financial crisis. One positive sign is the March 2000 interim agreement between PLN, the state-owned utility, and the Paiton IPP project, which will allow Paiton to start selling power to the grid. Indonesia's power sector is beginning to recover, with preliminary Indonesian figures showing strong demand growth in 1999.

- **Australia's** power sector is moving in the direction of integrated grids and a competitive power market. For geographic reasons, Australia still has isolated power grids in some areas, such as Western Australia and the Northern Territories. A project to connect the grids of Queensland and New South Wales was recently completed.
- **Singapore** is in the early stages of restructuring its electric power sector, which is intended to lead to a privatized, fully competitive market. Divestment of major state- owned power generation assets is expected in late 2001 or early 2002.
- **South Korea's** government has plans to split up and sell off the assets of the Korea Electric Power Corporation (KEPCO). KEPCO eventually is to be divided into six competing companies, with nuclear power plants kept together in one company.
- While about half of **Mexico's** electric power currently is generated from oil, plans call for most power plants built in the future to run on natural gas. Demand is growing rapidly, and there is some concern about the ability of the power sector to keep up with demand growth in the industrial sector. Estimates of the capital investment needed to keep pace with demand growth run around $50 billion over the next decade.
- The **United States** is in the middle of a transition toward an unbundled and competitive electric power market, separating generation from transmission and distribution. One major effect of this transition is the steep rise in generating capacity held by non-utility generators, and the decline in generating capacity held by traditional investor-owned utilities.
- **Canada** also is restructuring its electricity sector to facilitate competition. While more than half of Canada's current electricity supply is from hydroelectric dams, natural gas- fired power plants are expected to make up an increasing portion of Canada's electric power sector. The Canadian Energy Research Group has estimated that Canada's use of natural gas for electric power generation will triple over the next decade.
- **Canada** and the **United States** have highly interconnected power grids, and competition in the industry is expected to increase volumes of electricity trade between the two.
- **Chile** is attempting to diversify its electric generating capacity, which is heavily dependent on hydropower, after experiencing supply problems

due to a year-long drought in 1999. Natural gas is expected to grow rapidly as a fuel for electricity generation in Chile.

- **Russia's** electric power generation has dropped nearly 20% since 1992, as the Russian economy has contracted. Russia would like to increase electricity exports to countries outside the Commonwealth of Independent States (CIS) in order to strengthen the finances of Unified Energy Systems (UES), Russia's dominant electric utility company.

NATURAL GAS INTEGRATION
ASIAN REGIONAL GAS GRID INTERCONNECTION

- While natural gas trade in Asia historically has centered on LNG, pipelines may provide an alternative in the future. As a share of overall primary energy, East Asian countries consume far less gas than Europe or North America, in part due to the lack of an integrated international gas grid, but there has been discussion in recent years of building pipelines linking the region. Another idea would include a link to supply southern China and Chinese Taipei with gas from Southeast Asia.

APEC NATURAL GAS SNAPSHOT

- International pipelines currently under construction include one from the offshore Thailand Malaysia Joint Development Area (JDA), and another to bring gas from Indonesia's Natuna gas field to Singapore.
- The proposed Asian Gas Grid (AGG) project, with an estimated cost of around $8 billion, would link the Natuna gas field to Shanghai, China and tie in existing gas networks in Malaysia, Indonesia, and Thailand, and possibly Vietnam. With its projected rapid increase in gas demand, China could be expected to absorb the bulk of gas exported through the new system.
- LNG trade also has begun to expand once again following a downturn caused by the Asian financial crisis. India is to become a major consumer of Southeast Asian LNG once regasification terminals are completed. China also has held talks with potential suppliers of LNG for use in southern China.
- In Northeast Asia, discussions have taken place on the possibility of using Russia's natural gas reserves, the largest in the world. One scheme would deliver gas from Sakhalin Island to Japan through a subsea pipeline. Another would pipe Siberian gas to consumers in northern China. Internally, China is planning to develop a pipeline from the western Xinjiang province to Shanghai.

North American Gas Integration

- As natural gas demand in the United States has grown, U.S. imports from Canada have grown rapidly, and the gas pipeline networks of the two countries have become increasingly interconnected. This is especially true of the Northeast United States and the Pacific Coast, where Canadian gas makes up a significant portion of gas supplies. The United States received 3.3 Tcf of natural gas from Canada in 1999, more than half of Canada's total natural gas production.
- The Alliance pipeline, scheduled for completion in late 2000, will carry 1.3 Bcf per day of gas from Western Canada to the Chicago area. The TransCanada pipeline also will bring 900 Mmcf/d of new capacity to Chicago, which is set to become a major supply hub for imports of Canadian gas into the United States.

- The Maritimes and Northeast (M&N) pipeline, with a capacity of 530 Mmcf/d, will bring gas from the Sable Island field off Nova Scotia to customers in the northeastern United States.
- Increased natural gas trade between the United States and Canada has been, in part, a result of the deregulation of the two countries' natural gas industries.
- There are also gas pipeline interconnections between the United States and Mexico, which support a smaller volume of natural gas trade, in both directions. The United States exported 64 Bcf of natural gas to Mexico in 1999, while importing 55 Bcf.

Gas Pipeline Construction

ENERGY INDUSTRY PRIVATIZATION AND RESTRUCTURING

- **China's** petroleum industry is going through a major restructuring. As part of that process, China reorganized most state-owned oil and gas assets in 1998 into two vertically integrated firms, the China National

Petroleum Corporation (CNPC) and the China Petrochemical Corporation (Sinopec). Originally, CNPC had been involved mainly in upstream production and exploration activities, while Sinopec was involved mainly in downstream refining and distribution. The reorganization carried out in 1998 provided for a transfer of assets between the two, transforming them into vertically integrated regional entities, with CNPC in the north and west and Sinopec in the south. Sinopec transferred four northern refineries to CNPC, and CNPC transferred eight southern oil fields to Sinopec. CNPC still has a disporportionate share of oil production capacity, with 2.20 million bbl/d, compared to Sinopec's 0.75 million bbl/d. Refining capacity remains tilted toward Sinopec, with CNPC at 2.05 million bbl/d and Sinopec at 2.45 million bbl/d.

- CNPC in 1999 formed a holding company, PetroChina, including most of its assets for the purpose of offering shares on the international market. In April 2000, the company made an initial public offering (IPO) on the New York and Hong Kong stock exchanges.
- **South Korea** has seen significant changes in its downstream oil industry since the beginning of the Asian financial crisis. The South Korean government deregulated the petroleum industry in October 1998, and large conglomerates have sold off petroleum refining and distribution assets which were not considered part of their core businesses.
- **Japan's** downstream petroleum industry is undergoing a period of consolidation in the face of stagnant petroleum products demand and low refining margins. Several Japanese oil companies and subsidiaries of multinationals have announced strategic alliances or mergers in an attempt to cut operating costs.
- In **Indonesia**, the state oil and gas firm Pertamina is undergoing reforms under the new administration of President Wahid. In February 2000, a new president was appointed for the firm, and many senior managers were replaced. The Indonesian government has reportedly been considering reforms which would eventually end Pertamina's monopoly, under which it is a required partner for foreign oil and gas firms operating in Indonesia.
- **Indonesia's** state power company, PLN, is continuing its efforts to strengthen its finances and settle disputes with IPP's. The company's finances have been hurt by a glut of surplus generating capacity.

- **Thailand's** government currently is planning to split up and privatize the holdings of the Petroleum Authority of Thailand (PTT), as part of the package of economic reforms agreed with the International Monetary Fund (IMF) in 1998. The privatization is scheduled to take place in 2001. Thai Oil also recently concluded a major restructuring of its debt to keep it in operation, after the decline in petroleum products demand severely reduced the firm's cash flow.

- The **Thai** government also is planning to privatize the gas-fired Ratchaburi power complex. Under the plan, the plant's employees would receive an ownership stake, and the state power grid company would retain a 45% equity interest.

- The **Philippines** undertook a deregulation of its downstream petroleum industry in 1998, ending most government price controls for petroleum products, and removing barriers to new entrants to the market. While some new firms have begun importing petroleum products and establishing retail networks in the Philippines, the market remains dominated by three refiners.

- **Canada** is in the process of deregulating its electric utility sector. Alberta was the first province to create a competitive market in generation, with location-based rates and a power pool for spot trading in electricity. Ontario's electricity deregulation plan represents part of an ambitious effort to integrate the Canadian and U.S. power grids into one competitive market, and to spur competition and exports of electric power to the United States. Ontario plans to have a $7 billion, competitive power market in place by November 2000.

- The oil industry in the **United States** is undergoing a period of consolidation, part of a global trend. The ExxonMobil merger in 1999 was the largest oil industry merger in United States history.

- The electric utility sector in the **United States** is undergoing a process of unbundling and deregulation. From a primarily vertically-integrated industry, it is moving toward a competitive system in which power generation, transmission, and distribution are separated.

ExxonMobil

- The natural gas industry in the United States also is undergoing a process of unbundling and deregulation in several areas. Consumers in some states already have a choice of gas suppliers, even while the local distribution company controls the local pipeline infrastructure.

International Trade

The APEC economies in 1998 made up about 42% of the total volume of world trade. Trade within the APEC region grew rapidly during most of the 1990s, averaging an annual growth rate of 11.3% during the period from 1992 through 1997. The five largest intra-APEC importers in 1997 were the **United States, Japan, Canada, China**, and **Hong Kong, China**.

Member Economy	Value of 1997 Imports from other APEC Economies in $1997	Average Annual Growth in Intra-APEC Imports Between 1992-1997
United States	$588 billion	10.0%
Japan	$229 billion	10.0%
Canada	$170 billion	9.5%
China (PRC)	$138 billion	14.9%
Hong Kong, China	$130 billion	9.0%

The five APEC economies with the fastest growing imports from other APEC economies during the period 1992-1997 were **Vietnam, the Philippines, Malaysia, Peru**, and **Chile.**

Member Economy	Value of 1997 Imports from other APEC Economies in $1997	Average Annual Growth in Intra-APEC Imports Between 1992-1997
Vietnam	$9 billion	26.3%
Philippines	$31 billion	22.8%
Malaysia	$66 billion	20.7%
Peru	$4 billion	16.6%
Chile	$10 billion	15.0%

The five APEC economies with the largest intra-APEC exports in 1997 were the **United States, Japan, China, Canada**, and **Chinese Taipei.**

Member Economy	Value of 1997 Exports to other APEC Economies in $1997	Average Annual Growth in Intra-APEC Exports Between 1992-1997
United States	$495 billion	11.3%
Japan	$328 billion	6.9%
China (PRC)	$240 billion	16.8%
Canada	$197 billion	10.9%
Chinese Taipei	$106 billion	9.4%

The five APEC economies with the fastest growing exports to other APEC economies during the period from 1992-1997 were **Vietnam, the Philippines, Mexico, Russia, China**, and **Malaysia** (tied with China for fifth place).

Member Economy	Value of 1997 Exports to other APEC Economies in $1997	Average Annual Growth in Intra-APEC Exports Between 1992-1997
Vietnam	$7 billion	28.6%
Philippines	$26 billion	21.3%
Mexico	$99 billion	20.1%
Russia	$17 billion	18.6%
China (PRC)	$240 billion	16.8%
Malaysia	$77 billion	16.8%

Most members of APEC also are members of the World Trade Organization (WTO). **China** currently is a candidate for membership in the WTO. The United States and China reached a landmark agreement in November 1999. Before entering the WTO, China still must conclude bilateral negotiations with a number of other WTO members, including the European Union. Multilateral negotiations on China's accession protocol also must be completed.

Several other regional trade groupings overlap with APEC. The **United States, Mexico**, and **Canada** are members of the North American Free Trade Agreement (NAFTA). The Association of Southeast Asian Nations (ASEAN) includes APEC member economies **Brunei, Indonesia, Malaysia, the Philippines, Singapore, Thailand, and Vietnam**. **Peru** is a member of the Andean Community. **Chile** is an Associate Member of Mercosur (Southern Market).

Chapter 5

APEC, EAEC, AND FREE TRADE IN THE ASIA PACIFIC*

Dick K. Nanto

INTRODUCTION

In November 1994, President Clinton and the leaders of the eighteen nations/states of the Asia Pacific Economic Cooperation (APEC) forum met in Bogor, Indonesia, and signed a declaration setting a goal to establish free and open trade in the Asia Pacific. Concrete details on this free-trade area are yet to be worked out, but the goal is for the industrialized economies in APEC to achieve free and open trade by the year 2010 and the rest no later than the year 2020. The United States supports the APEC process in order to facilitate trade in the region, promote economic cooperation, and discourage Asian nations from organizing into an exclusive trading bloc with Japan or China at its helm. Malaysia has proposed forming an East Asian Economic Caucus (EAEC), a subgroup of APEC, that would exclude nations from the Americas and Oceania.

---

* Excerpted from CRS Report 94-914 E. November 23, 1994.

STATUS OF ISSUE

The Asia Pacific region contains nearly half the world's population, 60 percent of the world's gross domestic product, and 40 percent of its trade. U.S. trade with APEC nations, even excluding Canada and Mexico, is 76 percent greater than that with the European Union. In the near term, Asian economies are expected to grow 50 percent faster than the major industrialized countries. Since the U.S. market already is relatively open, Americans stand to gain more from the lowering of trade barriers abroad than other countries have in further reductions in such barriers in the United States. Import duties on automobiles in Southeast Asia, for example, range between 30 and 60 percent compared to 2.5 percent in the United States. Each $1 billion gain in U.S. exports to Asia generates an estimated 19,000 U.S. jobs.

U.S. Merchandise Trade with APEC Nations/Groups, 1993 ($ million)

Nation/Group	U.S. Exports	U.S. Imports	Balance
Canada	100,190	110,921	-10,731
Japan	47,949	107,268	-59,318
Mexico	41,635	39,930	1,706
ASEAN	28,285	42,270	-13,985
China/Hong Kong	18,640	41,093	-22,453
Taiwan	16,250	25,105	-8,855
South Korea	14,776	17,123	-2,347
Australia	8,276	3,297	4,978
Chile	2,605	1,462	1,143
New Zealand	1,249	1,208	41
Papua New Guinea	50	98	-48
Total APEC	279,905	389,775	-109,870
Total World	463,611	579,261	-115,650

Note: ASEAN includes Brunei, Indonesia, Malaysia, Philippines, Thailand, and Singapore. Source: U.S. Department of Commerce.

As these dynamic Asian economies grow, U.S. exports there will likely become relatively more important, while the U.S. market will become relatively less important to their exporters. In many high-technology areas, moreover, the Asia Pacific economies comprise the cutting edge of innovation and competition. For the United States, therefore, institutional arrangements to further cooperation with those countries may become increasingly important while bilateral negotiating strategies may become less so.

U.S. trade deficits also are centered on Asia. In 1993, the U.S. trade deficit with APEC member economies of $110 billion accounted for nearly all of the $116 billion U.S. trade deficit with the world.

On November 15, 1994, the leaders of APEC met in Bogor, Indonesia, and signed a declaration setting the goal of free and open trade in the Asia Pacific region by the year 2010 or 2020. The declaration is a consensus, not legal, document. Concrete details are yet to be worked out, but the goal is for the industrialized economies (United States, Japan, Canada, Australia, New Zealand, Singapore, and possibly others) to achieve free and open trade by the year 2010 and the remaining economies no later than the year 2020. The free-trade area would not be exclusive in that benefits could be extended to non-APEC nations under what is termed "open regionalism." All eighteen members of APEC signed the declaration, although Malaysia submitted several reservations to it. The United States argued against allowing the additional 10 years for developing economies to liberalize, but this extra time was retained primarily at the insistence of China, South Korea, and Malaysia. APEC governments now face the problem of translating this goal of free trade into domestic political support in light of strong pressures for protection (particularly in agriculture, textiles, and automobiles) and criticism of trade practices by countries such as Japan and China. Some Americans, for example, question that China is qualified to reenter GATT, let alone into a free-trade area with the United States.

The proposal to establish free trade under APEC originated in reports from groups advising the organization. The Eminent Persons Group (chaired by C. Fred Bergsten of the Institute for International Economics) called for complete trade freedom in all goods and services by the year 2020, while the Pacific Business Forum, a group of business advisors to APEC, has recommended a faster timetable leading to free trade by the year 2010.[1]

In 1994, APEC also adopted a Non-binding Declaration on Investment Principles that laid out guidelines for freeing foreign investors from double

[1] Eminent Persons Group. *Achieving the APEC Vision, Free and Open Trade in the Ana Pacific.* Singapore, APEC Secretariat, 1994. 80 p.

taxation, red tape, threats of nationalization, discrimination relative to domestic firms, performance requirements, and barriers to transferring funds. APEC further agreed to explore establishing a voluntary consultative dispute mediation service to supplement the dispute settlement mechanism under GATT (General Agreement on Tariffs and Trade).

In 1995, the APEC Ministerial and Leaders* meetings will be held in Osaka, Japan. By then, APEC officials hope to have developed a detailed action agenda for reaching the goal of regional free trade. This is likely to include measures to lower tariff and non-tariff barriers, simplify customs procedures, harmonize standards, and identify other obstacles to trade. Japan will chair the meetings and has stated that its two additional goals will be to combine an increase in development aid in pace with liberalization of trade and investment and to create a more streamlined APEC secretariat.[2]

BACKGROUND

APEC began in 1989 as an Australian initiative (with implicit backing from Japan) in response to free-trade areas which had developed in Europe and North America. Originally intended to exclude the United States and Canada, APEC was to provide an institution and forum for consultation and coordination on economic issues of importance to East Asia and Australia/New Zealand. Ultimately, however, membership was expanded to include North America. The inclusion came about as Asian nations assessed their dependence on the U.S. economy and the United States took measures to thwart the development of an East Asian trading bloc centered on Japan. The Clinton Administration has viewed APEC as an important component of its policy of creating a New Pacific Community. It also may offer regional solutions to trade and investment problems that go beyond the GATT or proposed World Trade Organization.

The momentum in APEC along with Japan's reluctance to take more of a leadership role in Asia or risk offending the United States has temporarily sidelined a Malaysian proposal to form an East Asian Economic Caucus. This EAEC (discussed below) would include only Asia members of APEC.

Membership in APEC began with twelve but has grown to eighteen nations/economies: United States, Canada, Japan, South Korea, ASEAN (Association of Southeast Asian Nations — Brunei, Indonesia, Malaysia,

---

[2] Mussy, Eugene. Next APEC Host Japan Eyes Subtle Leadership. Reuters News Service, November 15, 1994.

Philippines, Singapore, and Thailand), Australia, New Zealand, and since 1991 the People's Republic of China, Chinese Taipei (Taiwan), and Hong Kong. In 1993, Mexico and Papua New Guinea were admitted as was Chile in 1994. Additional membership decisions have been deferred until 1996. The European Union has been denied observer status, while Guam has proposed that it be allowed such status.

APEC encompasses member states that are remarkably diverse. They range from the North to the South, from China with 1.2 billion people to Brunei with 300,000, and from industrialized nations such as the United States and Japan to growing economies such as South Korea and to poor nations such as Papua New Guinea. Governmental and economic systems, standards of living, culture, religion, languages, and education levels likewise differ from country to country.

APEC symbolizes post-Cold War relationships in which trade and investment have become an important pillar in the foundation underlying world peace and security. While trade still may be used as a punitive measure in U.S. foreign policy, it also has become a catalyst for change in countries with authoritarian governments or isolated markets. APEC promotes cooperation and trade among the nations of the Pacific Basin, encourages open trading systems rather than trading blocs, keeps the United States engaged in the region, and provides the Asia Pacific with a counterweight to the European Union. In response to APEC, the European Union has floated the idea of a trans-Atlantic free-trade agreement.

Despite the great amount of trade and economic growth in the Asia Pacific region, only three trading arrangements currently exist. The North American Free Trade Agreement is the largest, but Australia and New Zealand have an agreement for Closer Economic Relations, and the Association of South East Asian Nations has launched a free-trade area that is to reduce barriers by the year 2003.[3]

Even though no trading bloc comparable to the European Union or NAFTA exists in Asia, Japan and its neighboring Asian economies are building trade and investment networks that could develop into a powerful trading bloc, if organized. Japanese and Chinese production networks have been proliferating in East and Southeast Asia. Japan also has been increasing the percentage of its trade that is conducted in yen, although a yen bloc still seems quite distant.

Trade friction with the United States, moreover, has forced many of the Asian nations to diversify their exports away from the U.S. market and toward each

[3] Currently, the ASEAN Regional Forum (ARF) provides the largest pan-Pacific forum for discussing security issues.

other. In 1991, 33 percent of the exports from the APEC member economies in East Asia were absorbed in Asia, while 23 percent went to the United States.

APEC Activities

In November 1993, the United States hosted the APEC meetings in Seattle and gave it the impetus to go beyond mere talk to concrete trade and investment measures. The United States added a Leaders' Meeting to APEC which raised the profile of the organization and expanded the range of issues covered. The Leaders' Meeting operates much like any summit and provides an opportunity for APEC heads of state (Taiwan's President has not attended because of objections from China) to discuss regional and world issues. Although APEC, itself, confines its agenda to economic issues, the heads of state at the Leaders' meetings have discussed security (North Korean nuclear problems), human rights (in China and Indonesia), and other issues. In 1993, the support by APEC for concluding the Uruguay Round GATT negotiations placed pressures on Europe that hastened the signing of the final agreement.

The annual APEC ministerial is attended by foreign, trade, and some commerce ministers from member states. The chair of both the Ministerial and Leaders' Meetings is held by the host country. Management of substance is handled under ministerial direction through Senior Officials Meetings held three to five times per year. The State Department and the U.S. Trade Representative co-chair these meetings for the United States. APEC also holds meetings for ministers or officials dealing with education, finance, and small-business. In 1993, APEC created a small secretariat in Singapore with an Executive Director, staff, and a modest budget.

Most of the specific tasks facing APEC are being addressed in working groups that deal with economic issues of importance to the region. These include: (1) trade and investment data review, (2) trade promotion, (3) investment and technology, (4) human resources development, (5) energy, (6) marine resource conservation, (7) telecommunications, (8) transportation, (9) tourism, and (10) fisheries. The working groups focus on the cooperative aspect of APEC's mandate, although some of the working groups now are moving into facilitating economic activity and into some policy matters. Each working group has one or more shepherds (members) who have volunteered to chair the group and provide leadership.[4] In 1994, APEC formed the APEC Business Forum to provide a channel for private sector interests to be expressed.

The number of working groups has been capped at ten, but APEC has formed two important committees. The Ad Hoc Group on Economic Trends and Issues is preparing assessments of long-term economic trends and studies of specific issues. The Committee on Trade and Investment is exploring trade and investment liberalization in a manner consistent with GATT principles and is developing initiatives to improve the flow of goods, services, capital, and technology within the region. It also has been charged with increasing cooperation among members on key issues.

EAST ASIAN ECONOMIC CAUCUS (EAEC)

In 1990, Malaysian Prime Minister Mahathir proposed that Asian nations combine to form an East Asia Economic Caucus with Japan taking the lead role. Membership would include the six ASEAN countries, Japan, South Korea, China, Taiwan, and Hong Kong but not the Americas and Oceania. The EAEC would serve initially as a consultative forum but eventually could lead to liberalized trading and investment relations. In July 1993, ASEAN decided that the EAEC would become a caucus within APEC with direction to be given by ASEAN ministers. APEC, therefore, would bridge both NAFTA and the EAEC.

Under the Bush Administration, the United States opposed the EAEC, but President Clinton said at the APEC Leaders' Meeting in 1993 that, with respect to the EAEC, he favors efforts that increase regional economic cooperation and advance the economic interests of the people, as long as they do not close off economic opportunities for others.[5] U.S. officials have warned, though, that the United States still has difficulties with the EAEC but has not rejected it outright.[6] Asians, however, point out that both Europe and North America have trading blocs and other arrangements. Why should Asian nations be prevented from doing likewise?

Most of the support for the EAEC comes from ASEAN, although China, South Korea, and Taiwan have indicated their willingness to join. Southeast Asian nations are reportedly becoming impatient with Japan's reluctance to take a stand

---

[4] U.S. Department of State. *APEC Overview.* Briefing paper. April 8, 1993. p. 6.

[5] Tarrant, Bill. Mahathir Welcomes Clinton's Stand on East Asia Group. Reuters News Service, November 23, 1993.

[6] Corben, Ron. US Has 'Difficulties' With Plan for Asian Bloc. *Journal of Commerce,* February 24, 1994. p. 3A.

on the issue. Japan, however, is loathe to worsen relations with the United States[7] and is cautious about taking world leadership roles.

For U.S. interests, an Asian trading bloc could weaken U.S. leverage in trade negotiations, if Asian nations coalesce to pursue their own interests. Bilateral trade negotiations with countries such as Japan, China, and South Korea are difficult enough as they are without those countries forming a united front under the EAEC.

Given the goal of free trade in APEC by the year 2020, the threat that the EAEC might develop into a trading bloc is diminished considerably. The role remaining for the EAEC, therefore, would primarily focus on consultations and coordination.

[7] Oishi, Nobuyuki and Satoshi Isaka, U.S. Or Asia? At APEC, Japan Pressed to Show Hand. *The Nikkei Weekly,* November 14, 1994. p. 1, 23.

Chapter 6

APEC YOUTH SCIENCE FESTIVAL PROMOTES MUTUAL UNDERSTANDING*

Nadine Leavitt Siak

The Asia-Pacific Economic Cooperation (APEC) forum was established in 1989 in response to the growing interdependence among Asia-Pacific economies. Since then, APEC has become the region's most visible vehicle for promoting open trade and economic cooperation. But while APEC's most obvious goal is to sustain the economic dynamism of the region, it also has as its goal the strengthening of the sense of community.

The annual APEC summits have notably served as a world-class forum where leaders, bureaucrats and private-sector executives meet regularly to exchange ideas and advance common goals. APEC programs, however, also can bring ordinary people together to work on finding solutions to problems of mutual concern. This person-to-person sharing of views and experiences could eventually lead to a strengthened APEC economy-to-economy cooperation. In turn, such linkages could not only optimize overall economic growth, but also could further sustainable development, improve standards of living, enhance public health, and spur scientific development.

---

* Excerpted from the Washington File. The Washington file is a product of the Office of International Information Programs, U.S. Department of State. Web site: http://usinfo.state.gov http://usembassy-australia.state.gov/hyper/2002/0422/epf110.htm

One example of successful APEC networking on an ordinary level is the APEC Youth Science Festival (AYSF). The stated goal of the AYSF is to raise youths' awareness of science and technology, based on the belief that such an awareness will consequently benefit the region's development. One of the most tangible results of these festivals, however, has been the opportunities they have afforded students and educators from different countries to learn from -- and about -- each other.

The first AYSF was held in Korea in 1998, with more than 500 students and chaperones/educators participating. The second festival, held in Singapore for two weeks in the summer of 2000, was attended by 582 high school students and 221 chaperones/educators from 14 APEC economies. The participants' schedules have included lectures given by eminent scientists -- including Nobel Prize winners -- home-stays, student summit science seminars, and visits to research centers and institutes of higher learning. Educational activities have focused on topics such as globalization, global warming, diseases, genetic engineering and clean environments.

The exact dates and location of the third AYSF have not been decided yet, but the festival may take place in either July or August of 2003.

Of the 558 students and chaperones/educators who participated in an evaluation of the second AYSF, approximately 95 percent of the respondents in the survey said the most beneficial aspect of the festival was that it allowed them the opportunity to make new friends, with the second most beneficial aspect being the opportunities provided to exchange knowledge of science and technology.

Zachary Gerson, a member of the U.S. delegation to the second AYSF, described the experience in an essay he wrote for the American Association for the Advancement of Science: "The APEC Youth Science Festival brought together incredible students, from many countries, with similar interests and put them in a positive situation where bonding across cultures was not only possible but inevitable."

Rebecca Kozizta, another U.S. delegation member, said she left Singapore with "an enhanced cultural awareness, a greater understanding of the international scientific community, a wealth of knowledge, as well as numerous life-long friendships."

"This festival has opened my eyes to the immense worldwide web of people and ideas," Kozizta added, "[and] has also made me aware of my desire to pursue an international science career that allows me to collaborate with scientists from around the world."

For some parts of the festival, the chaperones/educators attended a separate program, which comprised school visits, presentation of papers on science education in their economies, and a Science Teachers' Seminar.

One chaperone/educator on the U.S. delegation for the second ASYF, Ann Gattis, said she and others shared teaching materials at the festival and learned that, as teachers, they "have many of the same problems and share in the same joys."

"I have no doubt that if more people in our country shared in this type of experience there would be much less, if any, prejudice between us and other countries," Gattis said.

Another U.S. chaperone/educator, Claudette Bradley, is the director of a Alaskan summer camp program where Native American students are taught traditional activities by tribal elders while also engaging in scientific research projects. While in Singapore, Bradley spoke with other AYSF chaperones/educators about these Alaskan culture-based science camps.

While there may seem to be a world of difference between Alaska and, say, Australia, Bradley found that not only did other chaperones/educators show "great interest" in the U.S. programs, but several expressed interest in developing student exchange programs with the culture-based camps in Alaska and summer programs in their own countries. As a result of this networking experience, four students and two adult chaperones/educators from the People's Republic of China will be joining American Indian and Eskimo students for one of Bradley's summer camps in Fairbanks, Alaska.

In describing the AYSF program, Gattis concluded with sentiments that sum up the whole APEC cooperative philosophy.

"We have much that we can learn from each other," she said.

Chapter 7

ASIA PACIFIC ECONOMIC COOPERATION (APEC) AND THE 2000 SUMMIT IN BRUNEI*

Dick K. Nanto

INTRODUCTION

The Asia Pacific Economic Cooperation (APEC) forum is an association of 21 economies bordering the Pacific Ocean who are working cooperatively to reduce barriers to trade and investment, facilitate the exchange of goods, services, resources, and technical know-how, and strengthen economic and technical cooperation. In 1999, APEC's 21 member economies had a combined Gross Domestic Product of over $19 trillion and about 48% of world exports. The members of APEC have declared their intention to establish free trade and investment in the region by the year 2010 for industrialized members and 2020 for the others. For the United States, APEC has become a cornerstone of its economic policy in the region.[1]

On November 15-16, 2000, the Eighth Asia Pacific Economic Cooperation (APEC) Leaders' Meeting (summit) was held in Bandar Seri Begawan, Brunei (a country with a population of 330,700). In addition to the APEC summit, President Clinton held bilateral summits with several leaders of APEC countries, including

---

* Excerpted from CRS Report RL30688. Updated January 23, 2001.

[1] Roth, Stanley. Statement before the Asia and Pacific Subcommittee of the House International Relations Committee. September 30, 1997.

China, Japan, Russia, Singapore, and South Korea. Following the APEC meetings, Clinton traveled to Vietnam.

As a result of the bilateral summits, the United States and Singapore announced that they would begin negotiations on a bilateral free trade agreement,[2] the United States, New Zealand, Singapore, Brunei, and Chile agreed in principle to an "open skies" pact (eliminating restrictions on airline flights, prices, and routes among themselves),[3] and the U.S. and China announced that China would ban certain missile-related exports in exchange for a lifting of U.S. sanctions prohibiting Chinese launches of American satellites.[4]

In the Brunei summit, the APEC leaders reaffirmed their determination to realize the goal of free and open trade and investment among member economies and agreed on the need to expeditiously launch a new round of trade negotiations under the World Trade Organization in 2001. In a concession to developing country members (particularly Malaysia), the leaders called for a balanced and sufficiently broad-based agenda that would respond to the interests and concerns of all WTO members to be finalized as soon as possible in 2001. The APEC communique also stated that China should be accepted into the WTO soon, followed by Taiwan and sometime later by Russia and Vietnam; that the people in every economy should have access to information and services offered via the Internet by 2010; and that countries recovering from the 1997-98 Asian financial crisis should keep up with painful economic reforms even though their economies now are recovering.[5]

For Congress, APEC and the success of regional free-trade arrangements in various parts of the world have generated proposals for other bilateral arrangements among APEC countries.[6] In the 106th Congress, H.R. 1942 (Crane) would have encouraged the establishment of free trade areas between the United States and certain Pacific Rim countries. In the Senate, S. 1869 (Baucus) would have authorized the negotiation of a Free Trade Agreement with the Republic of Korea; S. 1870 (Baucus) would have authorized the negotiation of one with the

---

[2] See: CRS Report RS20755 (pdf), *Singapore-U.S. Free Trade Agreement*, by Dick K. Nanto. Office of the United States Trade Representative. U.S. and Singapore to Launch Negotiations for a Free Trade Agreement, Press Release 00-81, November 16, 2000.

[3] U.S. Department of Transportation. United States, Asia-Pacific Aviation Partners Enter Multilateral Open Skies Agreement. DOT Press Release 222-00, November 15, 2000.

[4] Perlez, Jane. China to Stop Selling A-Arms Delivery Systems. *New York Times*, November 21, 2000. P. A12.

[5] APEC Secretariat. Delivering to the Community, APEC Economic Leaders' Declaration, Bandar Seri Begawan, Brueni Darussalam. November 16, 2000. On Internet at http:// www.apecsec.org.sg.

[6] The World Trade Organization has been notified of some 120 free-trade agreements that have been put into effect.

Republic of Singapore, while S. 111 (Gramm), S. 1065 (Dodd), and S. 1871 (Baucus) would have authorized negotiation for the accession of Chile to the North American Free Trade Agreement (Chile is a member of APEC). These and similar bills may be reintroduced in the 107th Congress.

Among other APEC countries, free trade agreements have recently been announced or are under discussion among APEC members such as between Singapore and New Zealand, Australia, Japan, Mexico, Canada, and Chile and between Japan and South Korea. The ten countries of the Association of Southeast Asian Nations (ASEAN), Japan, China, and South Korea are considering an Asian free trade bloc. Since 1992, the Association of Southeast Asian Nations (ASEAN) has been phasing in a Free Trade Area (AFTA) for its members, although AFTA's goal is currently to lower tariffs overall and eliminate them only on certain items imported from other member countries.

APEC has become the primary regional institution in the Asia-Pacific for promoting open trade and practical economic cooperation. It is of interest to Congress because (1) it is becoming a vehicle for pursuing sectoral free trade and other initiatives similar in its longer-term objectives to what the North American Free Trade Agreement (NAFTA) is now; (2) the APEC Leaders' Meeting provides an opportunity for the U.S. President to raise and discuss issues with the heads of other APEC countries; (3) any concrete trade or investment measures developed under APEC that require a change in existing U.S. laws will need legislative approval and may call for fast-track negotiating authority; (5) the U.S. economy is linked to the economies of the Pacific rim through trade, financial investment, and direct investment in subsidiaries in the region; and (6) in view of the intense debate over the effects of NAFTA, the proposed creation of a free-trade arrangement that includes China, Japan, South Korea, Taiwan, Indonesia, Russia, Vietnam, and other Asian-Pacific nations is likely to be controversial.

U.S. financial support for APEC falls under the State Department's budget under Contributions to International Organizations and has required about $1 million per year. The goal of establishing free trade and investment among APEC nations is being pursued along three tracks. The first is through liberalizing trade in certain sectors such as information technology. These have been referred to the World Trade Organization in order to bring European and other nations into the agreements. The second is through bilateral free trade agreements, and the third is through incremental movements toward achieving the Bogor free trade goal.

BACKGROUND

APEC began in 1989 as an Australian initiative in recognition of the growing interdependence among Asia-Pacific economies and in response to the free-trade areas which had developed in Europe and North America. Originally intended to exclude the United States and Canada, APEC was to provide an institution and forum for consultation and coordination on economic issues of importance to East Asia and Australia/New Zealand. Ultimately, membership was opened to countries in the Americas.

Membership in APEC initially included twelve countries but grew to twenty-one. The founding members were the United States, Canada, Japan, South Korea, ASEAN (Brunei, Indonesia, Malaysia, Philippines, Singapore, and Thailand, but not Vietnam), Australia, and New Zealand. In 1991, the People's Republic of China, Taiwan, and Hong Kong joined. In 1993, Mexico and Papua New Guinea were admitted, as was Chile in 1994. In 1997, APEC extended membership to Peru, Russia, and Vietnam (who became members in 1998) and declared a ten-year period of consolidation before additional applications would be considered.

APEC symbolizes post-Cold War relationships in which trade and investment have become important pillars in the foundation of international relations and security. In many countries, international trade and investments have become a catalyst for change and an engine of economic development and modernization.

The objectives of APEC are:

- to sustain growth and development of the region;
- to encourage the flow of goods, services, capital, and technology;
- to develop and strengthen the multilateral trading system; and
- to reduce barriers to trade in goods and services and investment.

APEC's principles of operation are:

- that APEC is a voluntary association in which participants do not cede powers of regulation or enforcement to a supra-national institution;
- that decisions are based on consensus; and
- that decisions are implemented by individual members on a voluntary basis and by collective actions (the voluntary actions are coordinated and aimed at accomplishing a common goal).

At the 1994 summit in Bogor, Indonesia, APEC leaders signed a declaration setting the goal of free and open trade and investment in APEC. The industrialized economies (United States, Japan, Canada, Australia, New Zealand, Singapore, and possibly others) are to achieve the goal by the year 2010 and the remaining economies to do so by 2020. The United States argued against allowing the additional 10 years for developing economies, but this provision was retained primarily at the insistence of China, South Korea, and Malaysia. The Bogor Declaration is a consensus, not a legal, document.

APEC is nowhere near as far along as either the European Union or NAFTA. APEC's goal of free trade is to be phased in over the next two decades. Only the framework now exists to lead APEC members toward that goal. APEC is not a negotiating body nor are its decisions legally binding on its members. The APEC process has been called "concerted unilateral action" in which a set of principles and guidelines are agreed to by APEC members and used to steer individual member actions. Rather than a trade bloc, APEC can be characterized as a building block toward greater trade liberalization and cooperation not only within the organization, itself, but in broader contexts, such as in the World Trade Organization. The APEC work programs are conducted on the basis of open dialogue with equal respect for the views of all participants. This consensus-based decision making tends to be slow and cumbersome.

When APEC began, many thought it would be just another "talk shop" and excuse for world leaders to travel and be photographed. The movement in APEC toward voluntary free trade and investment liberalization, however, has gone beyond initial expectations and seems to reflect a change in world economic circumstances and attitudes. The nations belonging to the World Trade Organization (WTO) already have agreed to reduce tariffs and eliminate most non-tariff barriers. For the industrialized nations, in particular, tariffs already are so low in many sectors that some argue that dropping them entirely would make little difference. Until the onset of the Asian financial crisis in 1997, many nations were discovering the advantages of free trade and unfettered foreign investment in the fast moving, consumer-oriented markets of today. A perception was developing that closed markets and unfriendly investment climates can cause economies to lose rather than create employment opportunities. Since the 1997-99 Asian financial crisis and ensuing slow down in economic growth, however, some nations are taking a second look at the costs as well as advantages of free trade and capital flows -- particularly short-term capital flows between wealthy and developing economies. Malaysia has imposed some controls on international movements of capital, and China's relative insulation from the financial turmoil is partly attributed to the controls it maintains on its economy.

In terms of U.S. interests, APEC promotes trade and cooperation among economies that have been the most dynamic in the world, encourages open trading systems rather than trading blocs, helps U.S. businesses to remain engaged in the region, and provides the Asia Pacific with a counterweight to the European Union. For the Clinton Administration, APEC, along with the North American Free-Trade Agreement and the World Trade Organization, form the architecture of an economic strategy that the Clinton Administration believed would create jobs and growth through exports and trade. In response to APEC, the European Union in 1996 initiated ASEM, the Asia-Europe Meeting which excludes the Americas.[7] At the same time, countries in the Americas are pursuing a free-trade arrangement that would stretch from Canada to Chile.[8]

Critics of APEC include those who (1) assert that liberalized trade and investment has been primarily a one-way street that benefits trading partners more than the United States; (2) are concerned that the U.S. President should not be meeting annually with the heads of state of countries with alleged human rights problems (for example, China, Indonesia, and Vietnam), and (3) place higher priority on environmental considerations than trade.

Until mid-1997 when the Asian financial crisis hit, the Asia/Pacific was one of the most vibrant economic areas in the world. Currently, the region is recovering from recessions caused by the crisis. The region is important to the U.S. economy because U.S. trade with the Pacific has long surpassed that with Europe. In 1960, East Asia accounted for only 4% of world gross domestic product (GDP). By the year 2000, as economies return to their growth paths, eastern Asia is accounting for about a quarter of world GDP. U.S. exports to Asian APEC members had been growing at nearly 10% per year, although during the financial crisis they fell. The opportunities for U.S. businesses in APEC are considerable, but obstacles remain. APEC supporters maintain that numerous opportunities exist in Asian and other APEC markets for U.S. firms.[9]

APEC free trade, however, could become a two-edged sword. U.S. firms may gain greater access to Asian and South American markets, but exporters from those regions also will gain more access to U.S. markets. This could hurt

---

[7] ASEM met for the first time, on March 1-2, 1996, in Bangkok, Thailand. It included Heads of State and Government of ten Asian Nations (ASEAN plus China, Japan, and Korea) and fourteen members of the European Union plus the European Commission. The initial purpose has been to allow the leaders to become better acquainted with each other in order to build a foundation for further and continued cooperation among the participating countries. For information on U.S.-EU trade, see CRS Report 97-734, *The Transatlantic Business Dialogue*, by Glennon Harrison.

[8] See CRS Issue Brief IB95017, *Trade and the Americas*, by Raymond J. Ahearn.

[9] U.S. Council of Economic Advisers. *Economic Report of the President*. Washington, U.S. Government Printing Office, 1995. pp. 230-31.

previously protected American industries. The sectors that potentially could be most affected include apparel, agriculture, and motor vehicles (notably, pickup trucks). These import-sensitive industries have opposed liberalized imports from Asia and Latin America. Also, in light of the intense opposition in the United States that existed toward granting China the routine trade privileges of normal-trade-relations (most-favored-nation) status and allowing it to join the World Trade Organization, the question remains of how Americans would respond to establishing free trade with that nation. Furthermore, given the hidden barriers to trade and investment in countries like Japan (close business relationships, interlocking corporate organizations, etc.), would free trade with Japan be a one-way street? Would Japanese exporters gain unlimited access to the U.S. market, while American exporters still would face a web of private trade barriers in Japan?

THE APEC STRUCTURE AND ACTIVITIES

The chair of APEC is rotated annually between the ASEAN and non-ASEAN members. Since 1989, it has been held in successive years by Australia, Singapore, South Korea, Thailand, United States, Indonesia, Japan, the Philippines, Canada, Malaysia, New Zealand, and Brunei. China holds the chair in 2001 and will host the Leaders Meeting in Shanghai on October 20-21, 2001.

The focal point of APEC activities is the annual Leaders Meeting in which the APEC leaders set goals, publicize them, and provide momentum for the process.[10] This is usually held in November of each year, and is attended by heads of state except for those from Taiwan (Chinese Taipei) and Hong Kong who send other representatives. The major APEC decisions are made at this meeting. The summit also provides a platform for and gives momentum to major APEC initiatives. The Leaders' meeting was initiated in 1993 by President Clinton who invited the leaders to Blake Island near Seattle. Although APEC confines its agenda to economic issues, the heads of state at bilateral meetings conducted before and after the summit have discussed concerns over international security, human rights, and other issues.

Most of the decisions of APEC are first considered in ministerial meetings. These include the respective ministers dealing with trade, finance, transportation, telecommunications, human resources development (education), energy,

[10] Bergsten, C. Fred, ed. *Whither APEC?* Washington, Institute for International Economics, 1997. pp. 3-4. Note: The Leaders Meetings are technically not summits because of Hong Kong and Taiwan whose leaders are not officially heads of state.

environment, science and technology, and small and medium-sized enterprises. The largest ministerial is the annual Joint Ministerial Meeting which precedes the Leaders Meeting. It usually is attended by foreign and trade or commerce ministers from member states.

Management of substance is handled under ministerial direction through Senior Officials Meetings (held four times per year). In 1993, APEC created a Secretariat in Singapore with an Executive Director, 23 officials seconded by member economies for fixed terms and a similar number of locally recruited support staff. In 1998, it had a budget of $7,551,139. U.S. support of APEC is appropriated under Contributions to International Organizations in the Foreign Operations FY2000 Appropriations bill (H.R. 2606, Callahan, 106th Congress) in the amount of approximately $1 million for FY2000.

Most of the specific tasks before APEC are being addressed in committees or working groups or expert groups that deal with economic issues of importance to the region. For implementing the Bogor declaration, the Committee on Trade and Investment plays the key role. Other committees are the Economic Committee and the Budget and Administrative Committee. APEC also has ten working groups which work on specific areas of cooperation and facilitation: (1) Trade and Investment Data, (2) Trade Promotion, (3) Industrial Science and Technology, (4) Human Resources Development, (5) Energy Cooperation, (6) Marine Resource Conservation, (7) Telecommunications, (8) Transportation, (9) Tourism, and (10) Fisheries. Each working group has one or more shepherds (members) who take responsibility for coordinating the work of the group.

In 1992, APEC formed the Eminent Persons Group (EPG) and charged it with developing a "vision" for APEC's future. In 1994, the EPG recommended that APEC establish the goal of free trade, and, in 1995, as it completed its work, it recommended ways to achieve that vision.

In 1995, APEC established the APEC Business Advisory Council (ABAC). ABAC consists of up to three members appointed from each APEC economy. It is to provide advice on implementing the APEC agenda and other specific business-related issues.[11] For 2000, ABAC has been focusing its deliberations on how APEC

economies can benefit from globalization. ABAC's view is that the APEC approach of market liberalization underpinned by capacity building is of special relevance to the challenge of how to prosper from globalization. APEC's liberalization and facilitation agenda assumes that growth can come through

[11] U.S. representatives to ABAC are: Ernest Micek, Chairman of Cargill, Paul Y. Song, CEO of the ARIS Corporation, and Seymour Sternberg, Chairman and CEO of New York Life.

globalization, whereas APEC's capacity building agenda focuses on the sharing of experiences and resources to enhance the ability of all sectors of society to benefit from participating in the global economy. Trade liberalization has to be accompanied by capacity building for all economies to prosper.

In 1995, the issue was raised of whether APEC should be expanded to include consideration of regional security issues. Until then, consideration of non-economic issues was confined to bilateral summit meetings surrounding the Leaders Meetings. APEC had carefully kept its distance from security matters for fear that such issues would cause divisions within the group -- particularly between China and other members, such as Taiwan, the United States, and Japan. Such divisions could thwart cooperation in achieving economic goals. The consensus in 1995 among APEC members seemed to be that regional security issues should be discussed in the ASEAN Regional Forum and other fora rather than in APEC.[12] The ASEAN Regional Forum usually meets after the ASEAN Ministerial Conference and, in addition to the seven members of ASEAN, includes the United States, China, Russia, Japan, South Korea, Australia, New Zealand, Canada, and the European Union. It provides the largest pan-Pacific forum for discussing security issues.[13]

THE 1995 OSAKA ACTION AGENDA

Before 1995, APEC declarations and other documents were general statements without specifics on measures to be taken. In 1995 at the meetings in Osaka, Japan, APEC members agreed to an Action Agenda that was intended to translate into reality the aims of APEC particularly the Bogor Declaration of achieving free trade and investment among its member economies by the year 2010 or 2020.[14]

The Osaka Action Agenda is the template adopted for APEC work to accomplish its three goals of: (1) trade and investment liberalization, (2) trade and investment facilitation, and (3) economic and technical cooperation. The Agenda laid out nine general principles for members to follow in devising a road map to reach APEC's free-trade goal. These general principles have been used to guide

[12] Moosa, Eugene. *Regional Security Remains a Taboo at APEC*. Reuters Newswire Service. November 19, 1995.

[13] U.S. Library of Congress. Congressional Research Service. *Regional Security Consultative Organizations in East Asia and Their Implications for the United States*. CRS Report 94-79, by Larry Niksch. Washington, 1994. 15 p.

[14] Asia Pacific Economic Cooperation. *The Osaka Action Agenda*. November 19, 1995.

individual APEC members in devising national Action Plans for submission at subsequent meetings.

The general principles in the Action Plan included (1) comprehensiveness [all impediments are to be included], (2) WTO-consistency [consistent with World Trade Organization rules], (3) comparability [comparable actions with consideration for different starting points], (4) non-discrimination [benefits to be accorded to all APEC members and also to non-APEC countries], (5) transparency [in domestic trade laws and regulations], (6) standstill [no increased protection], (7) simultaneous start-continuous process-differentiated time tables [all start together in a continuous process to achieve long-term goal], (8) flexibility [in dealing with issues arising from liberalization a controversial principle that some argue allows for import-sensitive sectors to be liberalized more slowly], and (9) cooperation [to pursue economic and technical cooperation].

The Agenda also outlined actions that APEC economies were to take in fifteen specific areas. These included both actions by individual members and collectively by APEC in tariffs, non-tariff measures, services, investment, standards, customs procedures, intellectual property rights, competition policy, and dispute mediation.

Each APEC member also announced initial actions for liberalization and facilitation of trade and investment. These actions represented the first wide-ranging initiatives of APEC members to speed up implementing their Uruguay Round commitments.

Since Japan hosted the 1995 APEC meetings in Osaka, it held the Chair and the responsibility to ensure that the APEC process of trade and investment liberalization continued. Japan, however, took this opportunity to lead a group (including South Korea, China, and Taiwan) of members who argued for a weak definition of comprehensiveness[15] and insisted on including a general principle of flexibility that might allow the country to placate certain import-sensitive sectors (particularly agriculture) by putting them on a slower timetable or possibly even excluding them from complete liberalization. The United States and twelve APEC members viewed the principle of comprehensiveness (coverage of all sectors) as vital to achieving the Bogor vision of free trade in APEC. In Osaka, APEC

[15] October 25, 1995, Representatives Doug Bereuter and Howard L. Berman along with 27 other Members of the U.S. House of Representatives sent a letter to Secretary of State Warren Christopher and USTR Mickey Kantor urging the Clinton Administration not to weaken its resolve to press for "the promised comprehensive and detailed agenda for implementing the Bogor Declaration."

members reached a compromise that allowed the comprehensiveness principle to remain unchanged but added the principle of flexibility.[16]

At Osaka, Malaysia also argued for making all APEC commitments "voluntary" (meaning that the free-trade target dates would not be binding). For the Bogor Declaration in 1994, Malaysia had attached its objections to establishing the goal of free trade and investment by the year 2010 or 2020. As a compromise, the word "voluntary" was added. The Osaka Leaders' Declaration stated APEC's resolve to "encourage...the evolving efforts of voluntary liberalization in the region," but the Osaka Action Agenda clearly declared under the comprehensiveness principle that "the APEC liberalization and facilitation process will be comprehensive, addressing all impediments to achieving the long-term goal of free and open trade and investment."[17]

APEC members also disagreed over the non-discrimination principle or what has been termed "open regionalism." Japan has pressed for the benefits of APEC trade liberalization to be accorded even non-APEC trading partners on a most-favored-nation basis. Japan's government had stated that it thought APEC should not be a trading bloc that discriminates against outsiders. The problem with such unilateral trade liberalization, however, is that it invites free riders and makes generating public support difficult. The United States favored benefits to be accorded non-APEC countries on a reciprocal basis which has been the basis for other negotiations.[18] In practice, APEC agreements have gone to the WTO for binding and global implementation with non-APEC members.

THE 1996 MANILA ACTION PLAN FOR APEC (MAPA)

For the APEC Leaders' Meeting in the Philippines in November 1996, the theme was "from vision to action" meaning that APEC members were taking measures to realize the goal of free and open trade and investment in the region. The APEC leaders:

- launched the implementation phase of the free and open trade and investment agenda,

---

[16] The flexibility principle reads: Considering the different levels of economic development among the APEC economies and the diverse circumstances in each economy, flexibility will be available in dealing with issues arising from such circumstances in the liberalization and facilitation process.

[17] APEC. *Osaka Action Agenda*, p. 1.

[18] Johnstone, Christopher B. *An Awkward Dance: The Osaka Summit, Japanese Leadership and the Future of APEC*. JEI Report, October 20, 1995. p. 12.

- delivered business facilitation measures,
- agreed to advance common goals in the World Trade Organization,
- developed ways to strengthen economic and technical cooperation, and
- engaged the business sector as a full partner in the APEC process.[19]

In concrete terms, the first task was to coordinate the individual and collective initiatives into a Manila Action Plan for APEC. This contained the first steps of an evolutionary process of progressive and comprehensive trade and investment liberalization toward achieving the goals in the Bogor Declaration and in accord with the Osaka Action Agenda.

APEC took each of the Individual Action Plans (IAP) by member economies and categorized them according to the fifteen issue areas set forth in the Osaka Action Plan. Although the APEC process relies on concerted unilateral liberalization and does not formally evaluate each IAP, there was considerable pressure placed on countries whose plans fell short. One of the principles of the process is comparability -- which means no free riding.

The APEC leaders also announced that APEC supported an Information Technology Agreement (ITA) that was then passed on to the WTO for global consideration and broader support. The agreement grew out of recommendations from industry groups in 1995 to the Group of Seven (G-7) industrialized nations. It was endorsed by U.S. and European corporate executives at a November 1995 Transatlantic Business Dialogue, further endorsed by the United States and European Union at the Madrid Summit in December 1995, and then supported by the Quadrilateral (U.S., EU, Canada, and Japan) Trade Ministers and the G-7 in 1996 before APEC decided to support it in November 1996. By the time it was considered by the WTO in December 1996, 14 states or customs territories were prepared to sign the agreement. The ITA provides for zero tariffs in more than 92% of information technology trade among its 39 signatory nations. The tariff reductions were phased in over the 1997-2000 period, although developing country participants have been granted extended periods for some products.[20] APEC played a key role in generating support for this initiative among the newly industrializing Asia-Pacific nations.

---

[19] APEC. *APEC Economic Leaders' Declaration: From Vision to Action*. November 25, 1996.
[20] See the Information Technology Agreement on the WTO website at http://www.wto.org.

THE 1997 VANCOUVER MEETINGS AND THE MANILA FRAMEWORK

The 1997 Ministerial and Leaders Meetings took place in November in Vancouver, British Columbia. As the leaders met, several of the Asian APEC members were coping with severe financial crises in which the value of their currencies had plummeted, the value of stocks on their equity markets had dropped, and many of their financial institutions had become insolvent.[21] The International Monetary Fund had already arranged support packages for Thailand and Indonesia and was in the process of doing the same for South Korea.

While the APEC professionals considered the Asian financial crisis a diversion from the APEC agenda for trade and investment liberalization, it added a dimension to a Leaders Meeting that would otherwise have been a rather humdrum event. Prior to the summit, the APEC finance ministers had met in Manila and developed a framework to deal with currency and other financial crises. The ministers rejected a Japanese-backed proposal to establish a separate Asian fund to provide financial support for countries coping with financial difficulties. This was endorsed by the APEC leaders.

The Manila framework included three elements. The first was a strong domestic response by each country involved to create an economic environment that can attract capital and maintain confidence including to strengthen its banking system. The second was a stronger response by the IMF that included adequate financial support up front to ease any liquidity crisis and to provide the confidence necessary to avoid instability. The third was a cooperative financing mechanism through which the countries of the region would, on a case-by-case basis, backstop IMF financial measures to ensure that adequate resources were available.[22]

At the APEC summit, the leaders also designated fifteen major sectors where the principal goal would be to achieve free trade (tariff elimination) within a short span of years but not later than the year 2005. This represented a restricted, but nevertheless significant, advance on the Bogor Declaration. Detailed market-opening plans were to be concluded by the first half of 1998 with the aim of beginning implementation in 1999. These Early Voluntary Sectoral Liberalization (EVSL) agreements would be patterned after the Information Technology

---

[21] See CRS Report RL30272, *Global Financial Turmoil, the IMF, and the New Financial Architecture*, (pdf) by Dick K. Nanto.

[22] Summers, Larry. Press Briefing, Vancouver, BC. November 24, 1997. Transcript available on World Wide Web at http://usiahq.usis.usemb.se/regional/ea/apec.

Agreement endorsed in 1996 at the Manila summit and later adopted by the WTO. Of the fifteen sectors, nine were chosen for action. Of these nine, six had been nominated by the United States. The nine sectors were: environmental goods and services, energy sector, fish and fish products, toys, forest products, gems and jewelry, medical equipment and instruments, chemicals, and a telecommunications mutual recognition arrangement. APEC was to begin immediately to complete the work on these sectors through finalizing the scope of coverage, flexible phasing, measures covered, and implementation schedule.[23] The telecommunications arrangement was concluded under the WTO in 1998.

The other six sectors that were to be considered later for trade liberalization were: foods, natural and synthetic rubber, fertilizers, automotive products, oilseeds and oilseed products, and civil aircraft.

Although these initiatives to achieve voluntary sectoral liberalization were begun by APEC, APEC members agreed to send them to the WTO in order to seek participation by the EU and other nations and to make the commitments binding. At the WTO, the liberalization of these sectors became entangled in the proposal for a new round of trade negotiations and has made little progress.

Each APEC member also submitted a 1997 Individual Action Plan that indicated measures taken and outlined how it intended to move toward the Bogor targets. Another area of focus for the 1997 APEC meetings was trade facilitation and other measures to lower the costs of doing business in the region. The ministers welcomed the achievements under what are called Collective Action Plans that lower costs and reduce barriers to the movement of goods and services, capital, and business people. They endorsed work in these areas, which included: development of the Blueprint for Customs Modernization; establishment of APEC Internet sites; progress on alignment with international standards; increased transparency for acquiring and using intellectual property rights; development of options to enhance the environment for investment; development of model mutual recognition agreements; principles to guide work on dispute mediation; improved mobility for business people (including the APEC Business Travel Card); providing Internet access to member country tariff rates; and development of guidelines for improving the tendering, approval, and regulatory processes for independent power producers.[24]

---

[23] APEC. *APEC Ministers on Early Sectoral Liberalization* (Annex to APEC Ministers Joint Statement).

[24] APEC. *Asia-Pacific Economic Cooperation (APEC) Ninth Ministerial Meeting Joint Statement.* Available on the World Wide Web at http://www.apecsec.org.sq.

The 1998 Malaysia Meetings - Sectoral Liberalization

The 1998 APEC Joint Ministerial and Leaders' Meetings were held in Kuala Lumpur, Malaysia. President Clinton had announced his intention to attend, but sent Vice President Gore in his place because of the imminent bombing of Iraq. At the Malaysia meetings, APEC leaders gave support to Early Voluntary Sectoral Liberalization (EVSL) which would reduce tariffs in nine key sectors (chemicals, energy sector goods, environmental goods and services, fish, forest products, gems and jewelry, medical equipment and instruments, toys, and telecommunications equipment) covering $1.5 trillion in global trade. The telecommunications equipment agreement had been signed at the WTO earlier but was included in the list.[25] Japan, however, refused to participate in the tariff reductions for the fish and forestry sectors and reportedly had offered financial assistance to other countries in the region if they also would back away from the initiative. Trade liberalization effort in these sectors had moved to the World Trade Organization for global consideration and legally binding commitments (as compared to APEC's voluntary actions).[26]

Two other issues dominated the APEC meetings in Malaysia. The first was the global economic turmoil that began in Asia in 1997. APEC Leaders declared that they needed to deal urgently with the financial crisis and committed themselves to pursuing a cooperative growth strategy with the following dimensions:

- Growth-oriented prudent macroeconomic policies, appropriate to the specific requirements of each of their economies;
- Expanded financial assistance from the international community to generate employment and to build and strengthen social safety nets to protect the poor and vulnerable;
- A comprehensive program of support for efforts to strengthen financial systems, restore trade finance, and accelerate corporate sector restructuring;

---

25 Office of the United States Trade Representative. *APEC Telecommunications Equipment Mutual Recognition Arrangement*. Press Release 98 - 58. June 5, 1998. On Internet at http://www.ustr.gov/releases/1998/06/index.html.

26 U.S. Information Agency. Transcript: *Barshefsky 11/13 Briefing on APEC Trade Issues*. On Internet at http:// www.usia.gov/admin/025/wwwhbar1.html.

- New approaches to catalyze the return of stable and sustainable private capital flows into the region;
- A renewed commitment to the Bogor goals of achieving free and open trade and investment within APEC; and
- Looking toward the longer-term, urgent work among themselves and with other economies and institutions to develop and implement measures to strengthen the international financial system.[27]

Prior to the APEC meetings, Japan had been urged by the United States and other industrialized nations to stimulate its economy in order to restore domestic demand-led growth, clean up its banking system, further open its markets, deregulate its economy, and do more to help its neighboring countries in crisis. In the weeks leading up to the APEC Leaders' Meeting, Japan did take three measures aimed at restoring its moribund economy and promoting growth in east Asian countries. It announced a stimulus package (its eighth in the 1990s) of public spending and tax cuts worth about $196 billion,[28] unveiled what it called the Miyazawa Initiative -- a package of support measures by the Japanese government totaling $30 billion to assist economic recovery in Asian countries,[29] and, jointly with the United States, announced a new $10 billion multilateral initiative aimed at revitalizing private sector growth in Asia.[30]

Another issue turned out to create quite a stir at the meetings in Malaysia. Malaysian Prime Minister Mahathir Mohamad, who hosted the APEC meetings, had been a severe critic of the APEC trade liberalization process. As the Asian financial crisis battered the Malaysian economy, Mahathir imposed currency controls and restrictions on capital flows to and from Malaysia and stifled dissent within the country.[31] The capital restrictions were in conflict with the goal of free trade and investment in APEC but had attracted sympathy from other nations that

---

[27] APEC. *1998 APEC Economic Leaders' Declaration*. On Internet at http://www.usia.gov/admin/025/wwwhkld.html.

[28] Sugawara, Sandra. "Japanese Set Plan for Economy." Washington Post, November 16, 1998. P. A21. Japan. Economic Planning Agency. *Outline of Emergency Economic Package*. On Internet at http://www.epa.go.jp/98/b/19981116b-taisaku-e.html.

[29] Japan. Ministry of Finance. *New Initiative to Overcome the Asian Currency Crisis*. October 3, 1998. On Internet at http://www.mof.go.jp/english/daijin/e1e042.htm.

[30] The White House. Joint Statement by President Clinton and Prime Minister Obuchi. November 16, 1998. On Internet at http://library.whitehouse.gov.

[31] For a summary of the controls, see Aziz, Zeti Akhtar. *Preparing for the New International Financial Architecture: Malaysia's Programme*. Speech at the International Conference on "Managing the Asian Financial Crisis: Lessons & Challenges" on November 2-3, 1998. On Internet at http://www.bnm.gov.my/spch/1998/1102.htm.

had suffered the flight of short-term capital. Mahathir also had his former Deputy Prime Minister Anwar Ibrahim (who had opposed Mahathir and certain of his policies) arrested on a "morals charge." In October 1998, Reps. Ben Gilman and Doug Bereuter urged President Clinton to seek a new venue for the November APEC summit because his attendance in Malaysia might be perceived as an endorsement of the "anti-free market measures" put in place by that country and as a signal that the United States approved of the arrest of Anwar Ibrahim.[32] At the APEC summit, no bilateral meetings had been scheduled between President Clinton and Prime Minister Mahathir, and Clinton's non-attendance because of Iraq had an additional muting effect. While in Malaysia for the Joint Ministerial Meeting, Secretary of State Albright met with the wife of the jailed former Deputy Prime Minister, and in a speech at a banquet hosted by Prime Minister Mahathir, Vice President Gore voiced sympathy for Malaysia's pro-democracy forces. Both of these actions brought strong negative reactions from Malaysian officials.[33]

THE 1999 NEW ZEALAND SUMMIT - END OF FINANCIAL CRISIS

On September 12-13, 1999, the Seventh APEC Leaders Meeting was held in Auckland, New Zealand. The 1999 APEC meetings occurred earlier than their usual time because the World Trade Organization's Ministerial Conference was held in Seattle on November 30-December 3, 1999. APEC wanted to complete its recommendations for the WTO with enough time for them to be considered for the WTO meetings. The APEC leaders endorsed the launching of a new WTO round of multilateral trade negotiations and agreed that the new round of trade negotiations should: (1) include industrial tariffs as well as mandated negotiations on services and agriculture, (2) lead to timely and effective improvements in market access to the benefit of all participants, particularly developing countries, (3) have a balanced and sufficiently broad-based agenda, and (4) be concluded within three years as a single package but which would not preclude the possibility of early results on a provisional basis. For the new WTO round, the APEC leaders also: (5) supported the abolition of agricultural export subsidies and unjustifiable export restrictions, (6) agreed that the current moratorium on duties on electronic commerce should be extended, and (7) endorsed efforts to achieve

---

[32] "Gilman, Bereuter Urge Clinton to Boycott APEC Summit in Malaysia." Inside U.S. Trade, October 30, 1998. Internet edition at http://www.insidetrade.com.

[33] Blustein, Paul. "Gore Remarks Anger Malaysian Leaders." Washington Post. November 17, 1998. P. A29.

an agreement on transparency in government procurement. The leaders also agreed to continue working on the eight sectors designated for accelerated tariff liberalization in the WTO with the goal (not attained) of completed agreements in 1999.[34]

The problem of Japan's protection of its rice farmers arose at APEC 99. Japan and some other APEC members insisted that APEC support the position in the WTO trade negotiations that the agreements for all sectors be concluded in one package rather than have separate sectoral agreements implemented after they were concluded. The United States preferred separate sectoral agreements in order that the eight sectors designated for early voluntary sectoral liberalization by APEC in 1998 and other action on freeing trade in certain sectors could go forward without waiting for the end of the WTO trade round. Japan, however, was under pressure from its farmers not to open its rice market. It reportedly felt that the more products that were covered by the negotiations, the less attention would be drawn to its high rice import tariffs - which perhaps could be hidden among all the other items on the negotiating agenda.[35] Also, by not allowing agreements in sectors to go forward before the conclusion of the round, there would be less chance that an agreement on agriculture could be concluded early.

The APEC summit occurred at a time of increasing violence in East Timor following its vote for independence from Indonesia. Because APEC is an economic organization, the official APEC agenda did not address the situation in East Timor, but APEC leaders took advantage of side meetings with each other to put pressure on Indonesia to allow international peacekeepers into the country. While APEC was in session, Indonesian President Habibie bowed to international pressure and agreed to allow a United Nations peacekeeping force into East Timor.[36]

The APEC summit also occurred when the Asian economies appeared to be recovering from the economic crisis that had beset the region and certain other nations of the world since July 1997. As Thailand, Indonesia, the Philippines, South Korea, Japan, Hong Kong, and other Asian countries dropped into recession, their enthusiasm for further opening of their markets had waned. However, with the exception of Indonesia, the APEC economies seemed to have

---

[34] APEC Secretariat. Leaders' Declaration - New Zealand. Press Release 47/99, September 13, 1999. On Internet at http://www/apecsec.org.sq. U.S. Trade Representative. *Statement of United States Trade Representative Charlene Barshefsky at the Conclusion of the APEC Ministerial Sessions in Auckland, New Zealand.* Press Release 99-73, September 10, 1999.

[35] Shimizu, Yasumasa. "Rich Issue Again Raising Global Hackles." Nikkei Weekly, August 30, 1999. p. 3.

[36] Richburg, Keith B. "Jakarta Asks U.N. Force to End E. Timor Turmoil." Washington Post, September 13, 1999. p. 1A.

turned the corner, and there was heightened recognition that open, transparent, and well-governed markets were key to a return to sustained economic growth and prosperity. The general assessment of APEC's ability to cope with the Asian financial crisis, however, seemed to be that it really did little substantive work and that the International Monetary Fund, World Bank, the U.S. Treasury, and other players in international financial markets carried the burden of coping with the crisis.[37] In order to bring APEC finance ministers more into the mainstream of APEC activities, the finance ministerial meeting was moved to the period immediately preceding the Leaders meeting. The finance ministers did approve a work program that included specific proposals for implementing a voluntary plan to support freer trade and capital flows, compiling a compendium of international standards to strengthen financial systems, to work on insolvency law reforms, and enhanced supervision of financial markets.[38]

At New Zealand, the meeting between President Clinton and China's President Jiang, Zemin gave impetus to talks on China's accession to the WTO which had been suspended following the bombing of the Chinese embassy in Belgrade, Yugoslavia. The two also discussed Taiwan's alleged "pro-independence gambit" and North Korea and human rights issues.[39]

CONCLUSION

APEC is maturing as an organization and has now drawn most major players in the Asia-Pacific region into its membership. Its long-range goals are lofty, but it seems to be moving steadily toward achieving them. It is becoming a credible vehicle to discuss and coordinate issues in the region as well as to achieve trade and investment liberalization. The Asian financial crisis dampened enthusiasm for further trade and investment liberalization, but the crisis also underlined the need for market discipline in allocating financial resources. Market discipline occurs partly through liberalized trade and capital flows.

---

[37] See, for example, Sanger, David E. "Some Birthday Cake for a Toothless Wonder." New York Times, September 12, 1999.

[38] APEC Finance Ministers. *Memorandum to APEC Leaders*. September 6, 1999. On Internet at http://www.apecsec.org.sg/fora/activity_group/memo_apec.html.

[39] China's leaders have expressed concern over Taiwan President Lee Teng-hui's statement in July 1999 that Taiwan-China ties should be conducted on a "state-to-state" basis. See: Lam, Willy Wo-Lap, "Jiang to Pressure Clinton over Taiwan Stance." South China Morning Post. August 14, 1999. U.S. Information Agency. *The White House at Work, President Clinton: Key Achievements from the APEC Summit*, September 16, 1999. On Internet at http://www.usia.gov/regional/ea/apec/achiev99.htm.

The Individual Action Plans that are to bring the member economies closer to the APEC goal of free trade and investment in the region contain many significant actions. Most tariff reductions, however, reflect what the governments already are committed to do in the World Trade Organization. Some regulations have been changed in response to APEC efforts, but for most countries, only a few actions to reduce tariffs or ease foreign investment requirements have been taken specifically to achieve the APEC goals. The time has arrived when APEC members will have to consider concrete measures that go beyond those already scheduled in order to achieve the goals of the Bogor Declaration.

The sectors designated for early voluntary trade liberalization have been one way of going beyond the WTO commitments. Another initiative that has been suggested would be to adopt the APEC goals of free trade by the year 2010 or 2020 as a goal for the next round of multilateral trade negotiations under the WTO. This would put the rest of the WTO members on the same timetable as those in APEC. If the WTO members were to adopt this APEC goal, many of the problems now being debated within APEC would be solved. This includes the question of whether APEC trade and investment liberalization also would apply to non-APEC nations and whether APEC is to become an exclusive trading bloc.[40] The WTO, however, includes more countries than does APEC. This makes reaching a consensus to pursue such a goal more difficult to achieve in the WTO. The WTO also is attempting to pursue its own agenda for future negotiations.[41]

Another strategy that countries are pursuing to go beyond their WTO obligations is to negotiate free-trade agreements with other APEC members. In view of the difficulty in launching a new round of multilateral trade negotiations under the WTO and the slow progress under APEC, individual members are electing to go down the route of bilateral free trade agreements.

On the other hand, within the United States, opponents of free trade and investment argue that the U.S. should not pursue any more free trade arrangements because of human rights, economic, and other concerns. A question also remains about the extent that environmental and labor conditions should be included in such agreements.[42]

APEC is also facing the growing pains of any new organization. Some of its committees and working groups have overlapping interests. The number of

---

[40] Bergsten, C. Fred. "APEC in 1997: Prospects and Possible Strategies." In C. Fred Bergsten, Ed. *Whither APEC?* Washington, Institute for International Economics, 1997. p. 6.

[41] See CRS Report 98-841, *The World Trade Organization: Future Negotiations*, by Arlene Wilson.

[42] See CRS Report 97-291, *NAFTA: Related Environmental Issues and Initiatives*, by Mary Tiemann. Bolle, Mary Jane. *Labor Standards and Trade Agreements*. CRS Trade Electronic Briefing Book. http://www.congress.gov/brbk/html/ebtra25.html.

meetings is increasing, and travel requirements are rising for participants. Still, it has, so far, avoided forming a large bureaucracy such as those in the Organisation for Economic Cooperation and Development or the European Union. Also, it has expanded its scope to address financial problems as well as trade and investment.

For the United States, a problem related to APEC is that the U.S. merchandise trade balance with the member economies has been deteriorating. This can be attributed mostly to macroeconomic factors, but the political repercussions in the United States from this rising trade deficit could combine with specific trade disputes to have a negative impact on overall trade relations with some of the APEC countries such as China and Japan.

U.S. bilateral merchandise trade balances with the members of APEC show many deficits. As can be seen, the largest deficits are with Japan, China, Canada, and Mexico, all important APEC members. Out of a total U.S. merchandise trade deficit of $330.0 billion in 1999, $223.8 billion was attributed to just seven APEC partner nations - five in Asia (Japan, China, Singapore, Taiwan, and South Korea) and two in North America (Canada and Mexico). The total U.S. trade imbalance with APEC reached $253.5 billion in 1999. The imbalance in U.S. trade with the world, therefore, is primarily an imbalance with APEC.

APEC also raises some fundamental questions for U.S. policy. One is whether a U.S. consensus can be achieved on the APEC vision of free trade and investment in the Asia Pacific region or whether future trade liberalization will be confined primarily to multilateral trade negotiations under the WTO. Another question is whether the U.S. business community will continue to back the APEC process or whether they view the APEC goals of free trade and investment in the region as too long-term and too lofty to be actually achieved. A further question is whether fast-track negotiating authority should be provided to the President to cover negotiations under APEC. A final question is whether APEC is worth the effort and resources being devoted to it and whether the United States should continue to participate in it. These questions await a domestic policy debate over APEC that mostly is yet to occur.

Chapter 8

ASIA PACIFIC ECONOMIC COOPERATION (APEC), FREE TRADE, AND THE 2001 SUMMIT IN SHANGHAI[†]

Dick K. Nanto

INTRODUCTION

The Asia Pacific Economic Cooperation (APEC) forum is an association of 21 economies bordering the Pacific Ocean who are working cooperatively to reduce barriers to trade and investment, facilitate the exchange of goods, services, resources, and technical know-how, and strengthen economic and technical cooperation. In 2000, APEC's 21 member economies had a combined Gross Domestic Product of over $19 trillion totaling about 48% of world exports. The members of APEC have declared their intention to establish free trade and investment in the region by the year 2010 for industrialized members and 2020 for the others. For the United States, APEC has become a key institution for pursuing trade and investment liberalization and facilitation in the Asia-Pacific region.

On October 20-21, 2001, the Ninth APEC Leaders' Meeting (summit) was held in Shanghai, China. President Bush, Secretary of State Powell, U.S. Trade Representative Zoellick, and other U.S. officials attended. The Leaders' Meeting was preceded by an APEC Ministerial Meeting on October 17-18 and by a series

---

[†] Excerpted from CRS Report RL31038. Updated October 26, 2001.

of other meetings during the year addressing various economic issues.

For 2001, China hosted the Leaders' Meeting and, in consultation with other APEC members, set the major agenda items. The official theme for 2001 was "Meeting New Challenges in the New Century: Achieving Common Prosperity through Participation and Cooperation" with sub-themes of: (1) sharing the benefits of globalization and the new economy, (2) advancing trade and investment, and (3) promoting sustained economic growth. The war on terrorism and slowing world economic growth, however, dominated discussions. The leaders' statement on counter-terrorism was the first time APEC dealt explicitly with a non-economic issue. In the statement, the leaders condemned the attacks on the United States, committed themselves to preventing and suppressing all forms of terrorists acts in the future, to enhance counter-terrorism cooperation, and take appropriate financial measures to prevent the flow of funds to terrorists.[1] APEC leaders also reaffirmed the goal of achieving free trade and investment among APEC members and strongly supported the launch of the new round of multilateral trade negotiations under the World Trade Organization.

At the Shanghai meeting, the leaders also issued the Shanghai Accord in which they committed themselves to broaden APEC's vision for the future by identifying a conceptual and policy framework to guide APEC in the new century. The Accord included clarifying APEC's roadmap for achieving the free trade and investment goals on schedule with an assessment of overall progress in 2005, promoting the adoption of appropriate trade policies for the New Economy, following up on the APEC Trade Facilitation Principles, pursuing greater transparency in economic governance, and strengthening APEC's implementation mechanism.[2]

Representation by Taiwan at the Shanghai Leaders' Meeting became an issue when Beijing rejected Taiwan's choice of former Vice President Li Yuan-zu to attend. Beijing claimed that Mr. Li was not an economics official and consequently did not extend an official invitation to Taiwan to participate. The government of Taiwan refused to select another representative and ultimately boycotted the meeting.

APEC has become the primary regional institution in the Asia-Pacific for promoting open trade and practical economic cooperation. It is of interest to Congress because:

---

[1] Asia Pacific Economic Cooperation. APEC Leaders Statement on Counter-terrorism. Shanghai, China, October 21, 2001.

[2] APEC. APEC Economic Leaders' Declaration, Shanghai, China. October 21, 2001.

- it is becoming a vehicle for pursuing free trade and other initiatives similar in their longer-term objectives to the goals pursued under the North American Free Trade Agreement (NAFTA);
- the APEC Leaders' Meeting provides an opportunity for the U.S. President to raise and discuss issues with the heads of other APEC countries;
- any concrete trade or investment measures developed under APEC that require a change in existing U.S. laws will need legislative approval and may call for fast-track negotiating authority;
- the U.S. economy is linked to the economies of the Pacific rim through trade, financial investment, and direct investment in subsidiaries in the region; and
- in view of the intense debate over the effects of NAFTA, the proposed creation of a free-trade arrangement that includes the United States, China, Japan, South Korea, Taiwan, Indonesia, Russia, Vietnam, and other Asian-Pacific nations could easily become controversial.

The goal of establishing free trade and investment among APEC nations is being pursued along three tracks. The first is through liberalizing trade in certain sectors such as information technology. These have been referred to the World Trade Organization in order to bring European and other nations into the agreements and are categorized at the WTO as early voluntary sectoral liberalization (EVSL). The second is through bilateral free trade agreements or by encouraging multilateral trade negotiations under the WTO, and the third is through incremental liberalization measures (individual action plans) taken by APEC members.

Thus far in the 107th Congress, APEC is potentially affected by several legislative proposals. Some trade liberalization under APEC arguably will require trade promotion (fast-track) negotiating authority (H.R. 1446) and congressional approval. Several bills have been introduced that would authorize negotiations to establish freetrade areas with APEC countries. These include: S.138 and S.586 (with Chile) S.935 (with Australia), S.943 (with New Zealand), S.944 (with the Republic of Korea), and H.R.1566 (with Singapore, Australia, and New Zealand). H.Con.Res.73 requests that during the APEC summit, the President, call for the release of all Chinese political prisoners and Chinese ratification of the International Covenant on Civil and Political Rights. H.Con.Res. 194 calls for APEC to allow participation by Taiwan's President Chen Shui-bian in the

Shanghai Leader's Meeting. U.S. financial support for APEC falls under the State Department's budget (H.R.1646) under Contributions to International Organizations and has been $601,000 per year.

Debate over trade liberalization under APEC also is likely to address whether provisions dealing with labor and the environment should be included and whether the United States would be able to respond to foreign country violations of labor or environmental standards with economic sanctions. U.S. participation in APEC also touches on the broader U.S. debate over whether the United States should continue to pursue the expansion of international trade and investment with other nations – particularly through free trade agreements, the effect of trade and globalization on import-sensitive industries, and whether increased trade threatens or enhances U.S. prosperity, employment opportunities, and economic security. The Bush Administration has been approached by leaders from many other nations who desire to pursue free trade agreements with the United States. USTR Zoellick stated that the Administration will consider each of these offers seriously, while focusing on the Free Trade Area of the Americas. By moving on multiple fronts, he stated that the United States could create a "competition in liberalization that will promote open markets in the Western hemisphere and around the world."[3] The Bush Administration also considers APEC to be important because of its role in promoting trade and investment liberalization, increased transparency, openness, and predictability based on the rule of law, and discussion among national leaders. The Administration also is working with the International Monetary Fund in fostering rapid Asian economic recovery which is thought to mean more exports for U.S. companies and more jobs for Americans.[4]

The growth of regional free-trade arrangements in various parts of the world also has generated proposals for other bilateral arrangements among APEC countries.[5] Free trade or preferential trade agreements have been announced or are under discussion among APEC members such as between Singapore and New Zealand, Australia, Japan, Mexico, Canada, and Chile and between Japan and South Korea. The ten countries of the Association of Southeast Asian Nations (ASEAN), Japan, China, and South Korea are considering an Asian free trade bloc (ASEAN + 3). Since 1992, the Association of Southeast Asian Nations (ASEAN) has been phasing in a Free Trade Area (AFTA) for its members,

---

[3] Zoellick, Robert B. "Free Trade and the Hemispheric Hope." Prepared Remarks of Robert B. Zoellick, U.S. Trade Representative, Council of the Americas, Washington, D.C., May 7, 2001.

[4] U.S. Department of State. Bureau of East Asian and Pacific Affairs. Why APEC Matters to Americans. Fact Sheet, February 28, 2001.

[5] Currently, over 130 regional trade agreements are in force. Most provide for reduced trade barriers rather than free trade. Since 1995, the WTO received notifications of 90 agreements.

although AFTA's goal is currently to lower tariffs overall and eliminate them only on certain items imported from other member countries.

APEC Institutional Development

APEC began in 1989 as an Australian initiative in recognition of the growing interdependence among Asia-Pacific economies and in response to the free-trade areas which had developed in Europe and North America. Originally intended to exclude the United States and Canada, APEC was to provide an institution and forum for consultation and coordination on economic issues of importance to East Asia and Australia/New Zealand. Ultimately, membership was opened to countries in the Americas.

Membership in APEC initially included twelve economies (Hong Kong and Taiwan are not considered to be countries) but grew to twenty-one. The founding members were the United States, Canada, Japan, South Korea, ASEAN (Brunei, Indonesia, Malaysia, Philippines, Singapore, and Thailand, but not Vietnam), Australia, and New Zealand. In 1991, the People's Republic of China, Taiwan, and Hong Kong joined. In 1993, Mexico and Papua New Guinea were admitted, as was Chile in 1994. In 1997, APEC extended membership to Peru, Russia, and Vietnam (who became members in 1998) and declared a ten-year period of consolidation before additional membership applications would be considered.

The objectives of APEC are:

- to sustain growth and development of the region;
- to encourage the flow of goods, services, capital, and technology;
- to develop and strengthen the multilateral trading system; and
- to reduce barriers to trade in goods and services and investment.

APEC's principles of operation are:

- that APEC is a voluntary association in which participants do not cede powers of regulation or enforcement to a supra-national institution;
- that decisions are based on consensus; and
- that decisions are implemented by individual members on a voluntary basis and by collective actions (the voluntary actions are coordinated and aimed at accomplishing a common goal).

At the 1994 summit in Bogor, Indonesia, APEC leaders signed a declaration setting the goal of free and open trade and investment in APEC. The industrialized economies (United States, Japan, Canada, Australia, New Zealand, Singapore, and possibly others) are to achieve the goal by the year 2010 and the remaining economies to do so by 2020. The United States argued against allowing the additional 10 years for developing economies, but this provision was retained primarily at the insistence of China, South Korea, and Malaysia. The Bogor Declaration is a consensus, not a legal, document.

THE APEC STRUCTURE AND ACTIVITIES

The APEC chair rotates annually and since 1989 has been held by Australia, Singapore, South Korea, Thailand, United States, Indonesia, Japan, the Philippines, Canada, Malaysia, New Zealand, and Brunei. China holds the chair in 2001.

The focal point of APEC activities is the annual **Leaders Meeting** in which the APEC leaders set goals, publicize them, and provide momentum for the process.[6] This is usually held in November of each year, and is attended by heads of state except for those from Taiwan (Chinese Taipei) and Hong Kong who send other representatives. The major APEC decisions are affirmed and announced at this meeting. The summit also provides a platform for and gives momentum to major APEC initiatives. The Leaders' meeting was begun in 1993 by former President Clinton who invited the leaders to Blake Island near Seattle. Although APEC confines its agenda to economic issues, the heads of state at bilateral meetings conducted before and after the Leader's Meetings have discussed concerns over international security, human rights, and other issues.

Most of the decisions of APEC are first considered in **ministerial meetings**. These include the respective ministers dealing with trade, finance, transportation, telecommunications, human resources development (education), energy, environment, science and technology, and small and medium-sized enterprises. The largest ministerial is the annual **Joint Ministerial Meeting** which precedes the Leaders Meeting. It usually is attended by foreign and trade or commerce ministers from member states. Management of substance is handled under ministerial direction through **Senior Officials Meetings** (held four times per year). In 1993, APEC created a **Secretariat** in Singapore with an Executive

[6] Bergsten, C. Fred, ed. *Whither APEC?* Washington, Institute for International Economics, 1997. pp. 3-4. Note: The Leaders Meetings are technically not summits because of Hong Kong and Taiwan whose leaders are not officially heads of state.

Director, 23 officials seconded by member economies for fixed terms and a similar number of locally recruited support staff.

Most of the specific tasks before APEC are being addressed in **committees or working groups** or expert groups that deal with economic issues of importance to the region. For implementing the Bogor declaration, the Committee on Trade and Investment plays the key role. Other committees are the Economic Committee and the Budget and Administrative Committee. APEC also has ten working groups which work on specific areas of cooperation and facilitation: (1) Trade and Investment Data, (2) Trade Promotion, (3) Industrial Science and Technology, (4) Human Resources Development, (5) Energy Cooperation, (6) Marine Resource Conservation, (7) Telecommunications, (8) Transportation, (9) Tourism, and (10) Fisheries. Each working group has one or more shepherds (members) who take responsibility for coordinating the work of the group.

In 1992, APEC formed the **Eminent Persons Group** (EPG) and charged it with developing a "vision" for APEC's future. In 1994, the EPG recommended that APEC establish the goal of free trade, and, in 1995, as it completed its work, it recommended ways to achieve that vision.

In 1995, APEC established the **APEC Business Advisory Council** (ABAC) which consists of up to three members appointed by each APEC member. It provides advice on implementing the APEC agenda and other specific business-related issues.[7] For 2000, ABAC focused its activities on maintaining momentum in trade and investment liberalization, building capacity in APEC financial systems, and improving access to new opportunities through technological progress. In 2001, ABAC is expanding the work of its Action Plan Monitoring Committee and developing recommendations from three task forces dealing, respectively, with finance, technology, and trade and investment.

In 1995, the issue was raised of whether APEC should be expanded to include consideration of regional security issues. Until then, consideration of non-economic issues was confined to bilateral summit meetings surrounding the Leaders Meetings. APEC had carefully kept its distance from security matters for fear that such issues would cause divisions within the group — particularly among China, Taiwan, the United States, Japan, and Russia. Such divisions could thwart cooperation in achieving economic goals. The consensus in 1995 among APEC members seemed to be that regional security issues should be discussed in the ASEAN Regional Forum and other fora rather than in APEC.[8] The ASEAN

[7] U.S. representatives to ABAC are: Ernest Micek, Chairman of Cargill, Paul Y. Song, CEO of the ARIS Corporation, and Seymour Sternberg, Chairman and CEO of New York Life.

[8] Moosa, Eugene. *Regional Security Remains a Taboo at APEC*. Reuters Newswire Service. November 19, 1995.

Regional Forum usually meets after the ASEAN Ministerial Conference and, in addition to the seven members of ASEAN, includes the United States, China, Russia, Japan, South Korea, Australia, New Zealand, Canada, and the European Union. It provides the largest pan-Pacific forum for discussing security issues.

THE 1995 OSAKA ACTION AGENDA

Before 1995, APEC declarations and other documents were general statements without specifics on measures to be taken. In 1995 at the meetings in Osaka, Japan, APEC members agreed to an Action Agenda that was intended to translate into reality the aims of APEC) particularly the 1994 Bogor Declaration of achieving free trade and investment among its member economies by the year 2010 or 2020.[9]

The Osaka Action Agenda is the template adopted for APEC work to accomplish its three goals of: (1) trade and investment liberalization, (2) trade and investment facilitation, and (3) economic and technical cooperation. The Agenda laid out nine general principles for members to follow in devising a road map to reach APEC's free-trade goal. These general principles have been used to guide individual APEC members in devising national Action Plans for submission at subsequent meetings.

The **general principles** in the Action Plan included (1) comprehensiveness [all impediments are to be included], (2) WTO-consistency [consistent with World Trade Organization rules], (3) comparability [comparable actions with consideration for different starting points], (4) non-discrimination [benefits to be accorded to all APEC members and also to non-APEC countries], (5) transparency [in domestic trade laws and regulations], (6) standstill [no increased protection], (7) simultaneous startcontinuous process-differentiated time tables [all start together in a continuous process to achieve long-term goal], (8) flexibility [in dealing with issues arising from liberalization] a controversial principle that some argue allows for import-sensitive sectors to be liberalized more slowly], and (9) cooperation [to pursue economic and technical cooperation].

The Agenda also outlined actions that APEC economies were to take in fifteen specific areas. These included both actions by individual members and collectively by APEC in tariffs, non-tariff measures, services, investment, standards, customs procedures, intellectual property rights, competition policy,

[9] Asia Pacific Economic Cooperation. *The Osaka Action Agenda*. November 19, 1995.

and dispute mediation.

Each APEC member also announced **initial actions** for liberalization and facilitation of trade and investment. These actions represented the first wide-ranging initiatives of APEC members to speed up implementing their Uruguay Round commitments.

Since Japan hosted the 1995 APEC meetings in Osaka, it held the Chair and the responsibility to ensure that the APEC process of trade and investment liberalization continued. Japan, however, took this opportunity to lead a group (including South Korea, China, and Taiwan) of members who argued for a weak definition of comprehensiveness[10] and insisted on including a general **principle of flexibility** that might allow the country to placate certain import-sensitive sectors (particularly agriculture) by putting them on a slower timetable or possibly even excluding them from complete liberalization. The United States and twelve APEC members viewed the principle of comprehensiveness (coverage of all sectors) as vital to achieving the Bogor vision of free trade in APEC. In Osaka, APEC members reached a compromise that allowed the comprehensiveness principle to remain unchanged but added the principle of flexibility.[11]

At Osaka, Malaysia also argued for making all APEC commitments "voluntary" (meaning that the free-trade target dates would not be binding). For the Bogor Declaration in 1994, Malaysia had attached its objections to establishing the goal of free trade and investment by the year 2010 or 2020. As a compromise, the word "voluntary" was added. The Osaka Leaders' Declaration stated APEC's resolve to "encourage...the evolving efforts of **voluntary liberalization** in the region," but the Osaka Action Agenda clearly declared under the comprehensiveness principle that "the APEC liberalization and facilitation process will be comprehensive, addressing all impediments to achieving the long-term goal of free and open trade and investment."[12]

APEC members also disagreed over the **non-discrimination principle** or what has been termed "open regionalism." Japan has pressed for the benefits of APEC trade liberalization to be accorded even non-APEC trading partners on a

---

[10] October 25, 1995, Representatives Doug Bereuter and Howard L. Berman along with 27 other Members of the U.S. House of Representatives sent a letter to Secretary of State Warren Christopher and USTR Mickey Kantor urging the Clinton Administration not to weaken its resolve to press for "the promised comprehensive and detailed agenda for implementing the Bogor Declaration."

[11] The flexibility principle reads: Considering the different levels of economic development among the APEC economies and the diverse circumstances in each economy, flexibility will be available in dealing with issues arising from such circumstances in the liberalization andfacilitation process.

[12] 12 APEC. *Osaka Action Agenda*, p. 1.

mostfavored- nation basis. Japan's government had stated that it thought APEC should not be a trading bloc that discriminates against outsiders. The problem with such unilateral trade liberalization, however, is that it invites free riders and makes generating public support difficult. The United States favored benefits to be accorded non-APEC countries on a reciprocal basis which has been the basis for other negotiations.[13] In practice, APEC agreements have gone to the WTO for binding and global implementation with non-APEC members.

THE 1996 MANILA ACTION PLAN

For the APEC Leaders' Meeting in the Philippines in November 1996, the theme was "from vision to action" meaning that APEC members were taking measures to realize the goal of free and open trade and investment in the region. The APEC leaders:

- launched the implementation phase of the free and open trade and investment agenda,
- delivered business facilitation measures,
- agreed to advance common goals in the World Trade Organization,
- developed ways to strengthen economic and technical cooperation, and
- engaged the business sector as a full partner in the APEC process.[14]

In concrete terms, the first task was to coordinate the individual and collective initiatives into a Manila Action Plan for APEC. This contained the first steps of an evolutionary process of progressive and comprehensive trade and investment liberalization toward achieving the goals in the Bogor Declaration and in accord with the Osaka Action Agenda.

APEC took each of the Individual Action Plans (IAP) by member economies and categorized them according to the fifteen issue areas set forth in the Osaka Action Plan. Although the APEC process relies on concerted unilateral liberalization and does not formally evaluate each IAP, there was considerable pressure placed on countries whose plans fell short. One of the principles of the process is comparability — which means no free riding.

---

[13] Johnstone, Christopher B. *An Awkward Dance: The Osaka Summit, Japanese Leadership and the Future of APEC*. JEI Report, October 20, 1995. p. 12.

[14] APEC. *APEC Economic Leaders' Declaration: From Vision to Action*. November 25, 1996

The APEC leaders also announced that APEC supported an Information Technology Agreement (ITA) that was then passed on to the WTO for global consideration and broader support. The agreement grew out of recommendations from industry groups in 1995 to the Group of Seven (G-7) industrialized nations. It was endorsed by U.S. and European corporate executives at a November 1995 Transatlantic Business Dialogue, further endorsed by the United States and European Union at the Madrid Summit in December 1995, and then supported by the Quadrilateral (U.S., EU, Canada, and Japan) Trade Ministers and the G-7 in 1996 before APEC decided to support it in November 1996. By the time it was considered (and adopted) by the WTO in December 1996, 14 states or customs territories were prepared to sign the agreement. The ITA provides for zero tariffs in more than 92% of information technology trade among its 39 signatory nations. The tariff reductions were phased in over the 1997-2000 period, although developing country participants have been granted extended periods for some products.[15] APEC played a key role in generating support for this initiative among the newly industrializing Asia-Pacific nations.

THE 1997 VANCOUVER MEETINGS – THE MANILA FRAMEWORK

The 1997 Ministerial and Leaders Meetings took place in November in Vancouver, British Columbia. As the leaders met, several of the Asian APEC members were coping with severe financial crises in which the value of their currencies had plummeted, the value of stocks on their equity markets had dropped, and many of their financial institutions had become insolvent.[16] The International Monetary Fund had already arranged support packages for Thailand and Indonesia and was in the process of doing the same for South Korea.

While the APEC professionals considered the Asian financial crisis a diversion from the APEC agenda for trade and investment liberalization, it added a dimension to a Leaders Meeting that would otherwise have been a rather humdrum event. Prior to the summit, the APEC finance ministers had met in Manila and developed a framework to deal with currency and other financial crises. The ministers rejected a Japanese-backed proposal to establish a separate Asian fund to provide financial support for countries coping with financial

---

[15] See the Information Technology Agreement on the WTO website at [http://www.wto.org/ wto/ english/tratop_e/inftec_e/inftec_e.htm].

[16] See CRS Report RL30272, *Global Financial Turmoil, the IMF, and the New Financial Architecture*, by Dick K. Nanto.

difficulties. The Manila Framework was endorsed by the APEC leaders.

The Manila framework included three elements. The first was a strong domestic response by each country involved to create an economic environment that can attract capital and maintain confidence, including to strengthen its banking system. The second was a stronger response by the IMF that included adequate financial support up front to ease any liquidity crisis and to provide the confidence necessary to avoid instability. The third was a cooperative financing mechanism through which the countries of the region would, on a case-by-case basis, backstop IMF financial measures to ensure that adequate resources were available.[17]

At the APEC summit, the leaders also designated fifteen major sectors where the principal goal would be to achieve free trade (tariff elimination) within a short span of years but not later than the year 2005. This represented a restricted, but nevertheless significant, advance on the Bogor Declaration. Detailed market-opening plans were to be concluded by the first half of 1998 with the aim of beginning implementation in 1999. These Early Voluntary Sectoral Liberalization (EVSL) agreements would be patterned after the Information Technology Agreement endorsed in 1996 at the Manila summit and later adopted by the WTO. Of the fifteen sectors, nine were chosen for action. Of these nine, six had been nominated by the United States. The nine sectors were: environmental goods and services, energy sector, fish and fish products, toys, forest products, gems and jewelry, medical equipment and instruments, chemicals, and a telecommunications mutual recognition arrangement.[18]

Although these EVSL initiatives were begun by APEC, APEC members agreed to send them to the WTO in order to seek participation by the EU and other nations and to make the commitments binding. At the WTO, except for the telecommunications mutual recognition arrangement, the liberalization of these sectors has became entangled in the proposal for a new round of trade negotiations, and progress has stalled.

Each APEC member also submitted a 1997 Individual Action Plan that indicated measures taken and outlined how it intended to move toward the Bogor targets. Another area of focus for the 1997 APEC meetings was trade facilitation and other measures to lower the costs of doing business in the region. The ministers welcomed the achievements under what are called Collective Action Plans that lower costs and reduce barriers to the movement of goods and services, capital, and business people. They endorsed work in these areas, which included:

[17] Summers, Larry. Press Briefing, Vancouver, BC. November 24, 1997.

[18] APEC. *APEC Ministers on Early Sectoral Liberalization* (Annex to APEC Ministers Joint Statement).

development of the Blueprint for Customs Modernization; establishment of APEC Internet sites; progress on alignment with international standards; increased transparency for acquiring and using intellectual property rights; development of options to enhance the environment for investment; development of model mutual recognition agreements; principles to guide work on dispute mediation; improved mobility for business people (including the APEC Business Travel Card); providing Internet access to member country tariff rates; and development of guidelines for improving the tendering, approval, and regulatory processes for independent power producers.[19]

The 1998 Malaysia Meetings – Sectoral Liberalization

The 1998 APEC Joint Ministerial and Leaders' Meetings were held in Kuala Lumpur, Malaysia. Former President Clinton had announced his intention to attend, but sent Vice President Gore in his place because of the imminent bombing of Iraq. At the Malaysia meetings, APEC leaders gave support to Early Voluntary Sectoral Liberalization (EVSL) at the WTO which would liberalize trade in nine key sectors as APEC had proposed in the previous Leader's Meeting.[20] Two other issues dominated the APEC meetings in Malaysia. The first was the global economic turmoil that began in Asia in 1997. APEC Leaders declared that they needed to deal urgently with the financial crisis and committed themselves to pursuing a cooperative growth strategy with the following dimensions:

- Growth-oriented prudent macroeconomic policies, appropriate to the specific requirements of each of their economies;
- Expanded financial assistance from the international community to generate employment and to build and strengthen social safety nets to protect the poor and vulnerable;
- A comprehensive program of support for efforts to strengthen financial systems, restore trade finance, and accelerate corporate sector restructuring;

---

[19] APEC. *Asia-Pacific Economic Cooperation (APEC) Ninth Ministerial Meeting Joint Statement.* Available on the World Wide Web at [http://www.apecsec.org.sg].

[20] Office of the United States Trade Representative. *APEC Telecommunications Equipment Mutual Recognition Arrangement.* Press Release 98 - 58. June 5, 1998. On Internet at [http://www.ustr.gov/releases/1998/06/index.html].

- New approaches to catalyze the return of stable and sustainable private capital flows into the region;
- A renewed commitment to the Bogor goals of achieving free and open trade and investment within APEC; and
- Looking toward the longer-term, urgent work among themselves and with other economies and institutions to develop and implement measures to strengthen the international financial system.[21]

Prior to the APEC meetings, Japan had been urged by the United States and other industrialized nations to stimulate its economy in order to restore domestic demand-led growth, clean up its banking system, further open its markets, deregulate its economy, and do more to help its neighboring countries in crisis. In the weeks leading up to the APEC Leaders' Meeting, Japan did take three measures aimed at restoring its moribund economy and promoting growth in east Asian countries. It announced a stimulus package (its eighth in the 1990s) of public spending and tax cuts worth about $196 billion,[22] unveiled what it called the Miyazawa Initiative — a package of support measures by the Japanese government totaling $30 billion to assist economic recovery in Asian countries,[23] and, jointly with the United States, announced a new $10 billion multilateral initiative aimed at revitalizing private sector growth in Asia.[24]

Another issue had high visibility at the meetings in Malaysia. Malaysian Prime Minister Mahathir Mohamad, who hosted the APEC meetings, had been a severe critic of the APEC trade liberalization process. As the Asian financial crisis battered the Malaysian economy, Mahathir imposed currency controls and restrictions on capital flows to and from Malaysia and stifled dissent within the country.[25] The capital restrictions were in conflict with the goal of free trade and investment in APEC but had attracted sympathy from other nations that had

---

[21] APEC. *1998 APEC Economic Leaders' Declaration.* On Internet at [http://www.usia.gov/admin/025/wwwhkld.html].

[22] Sugawara, Sandra. "Japanese Set Plan for Economy." *Washington Post*, November 16, 1998. P. A21. Japan. Economic Planning Agency. *Outline of Emergency Economic Package.* On Internet at [http://www.epa.go.jp/98/b/19981116b-taisaku-e.html].

[23] Japan. Ministry of Finance. *New Initiative to Overcome the Asian Currency Crisis.* October 3, 1998. On Internet at [http://www.mof.go.jp/english/daijin/e1e042.htm].

[24] The White House. Joint Statement by President Clinton and Prime Minister Obuchi. November 16, 1998. On Internet at [http://library.whitehouse.gov].

[25] For a summary of the controls, see Aziz, Zeti Akhtar. *Preparing for the New International Financial Architecture: Malaysia's Programme.* Speech at the International Conference on "Managing the Asian Financial Crisis: Lessons & Challenges" on November 2-3, 1998. On Internet at [http://www.bnm.gov.my/spch/1998/1102.htm].

suffered the flight of short-term capital. Mahathir also had his former Deputy Prime Minister Anwar Ibrahim (who had opposed Mahathir and certain of his policies) arrested on a "morals charge." In October 1998, Reps. Ben Gilman and Doug Bereuter urged President Clinton to seek a new venue for the November APEC summit because his attendance in Malaysia might be perceived as an endorsement of the "anti-free market measures" put in place by that country and as a signal that the United States approved of the arrest of Anwar Ibrahim.[26] At the APEC summit, no bilateral meetings had been scheduled between President Clinton and Prime Minister Mahathir, and Clinton's non-attendance because of Iraq had an additional muting effect. While in Malaysia for the Joint Ministerial Meeting, then Secretary of State Albright met with the wife of the jailed former Deputy Prime Minister, and in a speech at a banquet hosted by Prime Minister Mahathir, then Vice President Gore voiced sympathy for Malaysia's pro-democracy forces. Both of these actions brought strong negative reactions from Malaysian officials.[27]

THE 1999 NEW ZEALAND SUMMIT – END OF FINANCIAL CRISIS

On September 12-13, 1999, the Seventh APEC Leaders Meeting was held in Auckland, New Zealand. The 1999 APEC meetings occurred earlier than their usual time because the World Trade Organization's Ministerial Conference was to be held in Seattle on November 30-December 3, 1999. APEC wanted to complete its recommendations for the WTO with enough time for them to be considered for the WTO Conference. The APEC leaders endorsed the launching of a new WTO round of multilateral trade negotiations and agreed that the new round of trade negotiations should: (1) include industrial tariffs as well as mandated negotiations on services and agriculture, (2) lead to timely and effective improvements in market access to the benefit of all participants, particularly developing countries, (3) have a balanced and sufficiently broad-based agenda, and (4) be concluded within three years as a single package but which would not preclude the possibility of early results on a provisional basis. For the new WTO round, the APEC leaders also: (5) supported the abolition of agricultural export subsidies and unjustifiable export restrictions, (6) agreed that the current moratorium on duties

[26] "Gilman, Bereuter Urge Clinton to Boycott APEC Summit in Malaysia." *Inside U.S. Trade*, October 30, 1998. Internet edition at [http://www.insidetrade.com].

[27] Blustein, Paul. "Gore Remarks Anger Malaysian Leaders." *Washington Post*. November 17, 1998. P. A29.

on electronic commerce should be extended, and (7) endorsed efforts to achieve an agreement on transparency in government procurement. The leaders also agreed to continue working on the remaining eight sectors designated for accelerated tariff liberalization (EVSL) in the WTO with the goal (not attained) of completed agreements in 1999.[28]

The problem of Japan's protection of its rice farmers arose at APEC 99. Japan and some other APEC members insisted that APEC support the position in the WTO trade negotiations that the agreements for all sectors be concluded in one package rather than have separate sectoral agreements implemented after they were concluded. The United States preferred separate sectoral agreements in order that the eight sectors designated for early voluntary sectoral liberalization by APEC in 1998 and other action on freeing trade in certain sectors could go forward without waiting for the end of the WTO trade round. Japan, however, was under pressure from its farmers not to open its rice market. It reportedly felt that the more products that were covered by the negotiations, the less attention would be drawn to its high rice import tariffs.[29] Also, by not allowing agreements in sectors to go forward before the conclusion of the round, proponents of the "single package" theory reportedly felt that there would be less chance that an agreement on agriculture could be concluded early.

The APEC summit occurred at a time of increasing violence in East Timor following its vote for independence from Indonesia. APEC leaders took advantage of bilateral meetings with each other to put pressure on Indonesia to allow international peacekeepers into the country. While APEC was in session, Indonesian President Habibie bowed to international concerns and agreed to allow a United Nations peacekeeping force into East Timor.[30]

The APEC summit also occurred when the Asian economies appeared to be recovering from the economic crisis that had beset the region and certain other nations of the world since July 1997. As Thailand, Indonesia, the Philippines, South Korea, Japan, Hong Kong, and other Asian countries dropped into recession, their enthusiasm for further opening of their markets had waned. However, with the exception of Indonesia, the APEC economies seemed to have turned the corner, and there was heightened recognition that open, transparent,

---

[28] APEC Secretariat. Leaders' Declaration - New Zealand. Press Release 47/99, September 13, 1999. On Internet at [http://www.apecsec.org.sg]. U.S. Trade Representative. Statement of United States Trade Representative Charlene Barshefsky at the Conclusion of the APEC Ministerial Sessions in Auckland, New Zealand. Press Release 99-73, September 10, 1999.

[29] Shimizu, Yasumasa. "Rich Issue Again Raising Global Hackles." *Nikkei Weekly*, August 30, 1999. p. 3.

[30] Richburg, Keith B. "Jakarta Asks U.N. Force to End E. Timor Turmoil." *Washington Post*, September 13, 1999. p. 1A.

and well-governed markets were key to a return to sustained economic growth and prosperity. The general assessment of APEC's ability to cope with the Asian financial crisis, however, seemed to be that APEC really did little substantive work and that the International Monetary Fund, World Bank, the U.S. Treasury, and other players in international financial markets carried the burden of coping with the crisis.[31] In order to bring APEC finance ministers more into the mainstream of APEC activities, the finance ministerial meeting was moved to the period immediately preceding the Leaders meeting.

At New Zealand, the meeting between President Clinton and China's President Jiang, Zemin gave impetus to talks on China's accession to the WTO which had been suspended following the bombing of the Chinese embassy in Belgrade, Yugoslavia. The two also discussed Taiwan's alleged "pro-independence gambit"and North Korea and human rights issues.[32]

THE 2000 BRUNEI SUMMIT – TOWARD BILATERAL FTAS

On November 15-16, 2000, the Eighth APEC Leaders' Meeting was held in Bandar Seri Begawan, Brunei. During the bilateral meeting with Singapore, the United States and Singapore announced that they would begin negotiations on a bilateral free trade agreement.[33] Given the stalled start of the WTO multilateral negotiations, more and more countries were opting to proceed with bilateral free trade agreements. During other bilateral meetings, the United States, New Zealand, Singapore, Brunei, and Chile agreed in principle to an "open skies" pact (eliminating restrictions on airline flights, prices, and routes among themselves),[34] and the U.S. and China announced that China would ban certain missile-related exports in exchange for a lifting of U.S. sanctions prohibiting Chinese launches of American satellites.[35]

In the Brunei summit, the APEC leaders reaffirmed their determination to

[31] See, for example, Sanger, David E. "Some Birthday Cake for a Toothless Wonder." *New York Times*, September 12, 1999.

[32] China's leaders have expressed concern over Taiwan President Lee Teng-hui's statement in July 1999 that Taiwan-China ties should be conducted on a "state-to-state" basis. See: Lam, Willy Wo-Lap, "Jiang to Pressure Clinton over Taiwan Stance." South China Morning Post. August 14, 1999. U.S. Information Agency. The White House at Work, President Clinton: Key Achievements from the APEC Summit, September 16, 1999.

[33] See CRS Report RS20755, *Singapore-U.S. Free Trade Agreement*, by Dick K. Nanto.

[34] U.S. Department of Transportation. United States, Asia-Pacific Aviation Partners Enter Multilateral Open Skies Agreement. DOT Press Release 222-00, November 15, 2000.

[35] Perlez, Jane. China to Stop Selling A-Arms Delivery Systems. *New York Times*, November 21, 2000. P. A12.

realize the goal of free and open trade and investment among member economies and agreed on the need to expeditiously launch a new round of trade negotiations under the World Trade Organization in 2001. In a concession to developing country members (particularly Malaysia), the leaders called for a balanced and sufficiently broad-based agenda that would respond to the interests and concerns of all WTO members to be finalized as soon as possible in 2001. The APEC communique also stated that China should be accepted into the WTO soon, followed by Taiwan and sometime later by Russia and Vietnam; that the people in every economy should have access to information and services offered via the Internet by 2010; and that countries recovering from the 1997-98 Asian financial crisis should keep up with painful economic reforms even though their economies now are recovering.[36]

POLICY ASSESSMENT AND IMPLICATIONS

Trade liberalization under APEC is nowhere near as far along as that under either the European Union or the North America Free Trade Agreement. APEC's goal of free trade is to be phased in over the next two decades. Only the framework now exists to lead APEC members toward that goal. APEC is not a negotiating body nor are its decisions legally binding on its members. The APEC process has been called "concerted unilateral action" in which a set of principles and guidelines are agreed to by APEC members and used to steer individual member actions. Rather than a trade bloc, APEC can be characterized as a building block toward greater trade liberalization and cooperation not only within the organization, itself, but in broader contexts, such as in the World Trade Organization. The APEC work programs are conducted on the basis of open dialogue with equal respect for the views of all participants – both the member countries and, to a certain extent, private business interests. This consensus-based decision making, however, tends to be slow and cumbersome.

When APEC began, many thought it would be just another "talk shop." The movement in APEC toward voluntary free trade and investment liberalization, however, has gone beyond initial expectations and seems to reflect a change in world economic circumstances and attitudes. The nations belonging to the WTO already have agreed to reduce tariffs and eliminate most non-tariff barriers. For the industrialized nations, in particular, tariffs already are so low in many sectors

[36] APEC Secretariat. Delivering to the Community, APEC Economic Leaders' Declaration, Bandar Seri Begawan, Brueni Darussalam. November 16, 2000. On Internet at [http://www.apecsec.org.sg].

that some argue that dropping them entirely would make little difference. Until the onset of the Asian financial crisis in 1997, many nations were discovering the advantages of free trade and unfettered foreign investment in today's fast moving, consumer-oriented markets. A perception was developing that closed markets and unfriendly investment climates can cause economies to lose rather than create employment opportunities. Since the 1997-99 Asian financial crisis and ensuing slow down in economic growth, however, some nations are taking a second look at the costs as well as advantages of free trade and capital flows — particularly short-term capital flows between wealthy and developing economies.

In terms of U.S. interests, APEC promotes trade and cooperation among economies that have been the most dynamic in the world, encourages open trading systems rather than trading blocs, helps U.S. businesses remain engaged in the region, and provides the Asia-Pacific region with a counterweight to the European Union. In response to APEC, the European Union in 1996 initiated ASEM, the Asia-Europe Meeting, which excludes the Americas.[37] At the same time, countries in the Americas are pursuing the Free Trade Area of the Americas (FTAA) a free-trade arrangement that would stretch from Canada to Chile.[38]

Critics of APEC include those who (1) assert that liberalized trade and investment has been primarily a one-way street that benefits trading partners more than the United States; (2) are concerned that the U.S. President should not be meeting annually with the heads of state of countries with alleged human rights problems (for example, China, Indonesia, and Vietnam), and (3) place higher priority on environmental considerations than trade.

Some import sensitive sectors also have opposed further opening of U.S. markets and more free trade agreements. They fear that APEC free trade could become a two-edged sword. U.S. firms could gain greater access to Asian and South American markets, but exporters from those regions also would gain more access to U.S. markets. There are concerns that this could hurt previously protected American industries, such as apparel, agriculture, steel, and motor vehicles (notably, pickup trucks). Some in these import-sensitive industries have opposed liberalized imports from Asia and Latin America. Also, in light of the intense opposition from some in the United States concerning granting China the

---

[37] ASEM met for the first time, on March 1-2, 1996, in Bangkok, Thailand. It included Heads of State and Government of ten Asian Nations (ASEAN plus China, Japan, and Korea) and fourteen members of the European Union plus the European Commission. The initial purpose has been to allow the leaders to become better acquainted with each other in order to build a foundation for further and continued cooperation among the participating countries. For information on U.S.-EU trade, see CRS Report 97-734, *The Transatlantic Business Dialogue*, by Glennon Harrison.

[38] See CRS Report RS20864, *A Free Trade Area of the Americas: Status of Negotiations and Major Policy Issues*, by J. F. Hornbeck.

trade privileges of normal-traderelations (most-favored-nation) status and allowing it to join the World Trade Organization, the question remains of how Americans would respond to establishing free trade with that nation. Furthermore, given the hidden barriers to trade and investment in countries like Japan (close business relationships, interlocking corporate organizations, etc.), some have questioned whether free trade with Japan might be a one-way street. Would Japanese exporters gain unlimited access to the U.S. market, while American exporters still would face a web of private trade barriers in Japan?

APEC is maturing as an organization and has now drawn most major players in the Asia-Pacific region into its membership. Its long-range goals are lofty, but it seems to be moving steadily toward achieving them. It is becoming a credible vehicle to discuss and coordinate issues in the region as well as to achieve trade and investment liberalization. The Asian financial crisis dampened enthusiasm for further opening of markets, but the crisis also underlined the need for market discipline in allocating financial resources. Market discipline occurs partly through liberalized trade and capital flows.

The Individual Action Plans that are to bring the member economies closer to the APEC goal of free trade and investment in the region contain many significant actions. Most tariff reductions, however, reflect what member governments already are committed to do in the World Trade Organization. Some regulations have been changed in response to APEC efforts, but for most countries, only a few actions to reduce tariffs or ease foreign investment requirements have been taken specifically to achieve the APEC goals. The time has arrived, however, when APEC members will have to consider concrete measures that go beyond those already scheduled in order to achieve the goals of the Bogor Declaration.

The sectors designated for early voluntary trade liberalization at the 1998 APEC summit have been one way of going beyond the WTO commitments, although this sectoral liberalization effort has been stalled at the WTO. Another strategy that has been suggested would be to adopt the APEC goals of free trade by the year 2010 or 2020 as a goal for the next round of multilateral trade negotiations under the WTO. This would put the rest of the WTO members on the same timetable as those in APEC. If the WTO members were to adopt this APEC goal, many of the problems now being debated within APEC would be solved. This includes the question of whether APEC trade and investment liberalization also would apply to non-APEC nations and whether APEC is to become an exclusive trading bloc.[39] The WTO, however, includes more countries than does

[39] Bergsten, C. Fred. "APEC in 1997: Prospects and Possible Strategies." In C. Fred Bergsten, Ed. *Whither APEC?* Washington, Institute for International Economics, 1997. p. 6.

APEC. This makes reaching a consensus to pursue such a goal more difficult and more unlikely to be to be achieved quickly. The WTO also is attempting to pursue its own agenda for future negotiations.[40]

Another strategy that countries are pursuing to go beyond their WTO obligations is to negotiate free-trade agreements with other APEC members. In view of the difficulty in launching a new round of multilateral trade negotiations under the WTO and the slow progress under APEC, many individual members are electing to go down the route of bilateral free trade agreements.

On the other hand, within the United States, those who question the expansion of international trade and investment often argue that the U.S. should not pursue more free-trade arrangements because of human rights, economic, and other concerns. Import-sensitive industries are among those who often oppose granting other nations greater access to U.S. markets. They also are less interested in access to foreign markets that might be accorded through trade and investment liberalization. Controversy also continues over the extent to which environmental and labor conditions should be included in such agreements.[41] Anti-globalization protesters who have directed their efforts mainly to oppose WTO, International Monetary Fund, and World Bank activities also could oppose further trade liberalization under APEC.

APEC is also facing the growing pains of any new organization. Some of its committees and working groups have overlapping interests. The number of meetings is increasing, and travel requirements are rising for participants. Still, it has, so far, avoided forming a large bureaucracy such as those in the Organization for Economic Cooperation and Development or the European Union. Also, it has expanded its scope to address financial problems as well as trade and investment.

For the United States, a problem related to APEC is that the U.S. merchandise trade balance with the APEC member economies has been deteriorating. This can be attributed mostly to U.S. macroeconomic conditions, but the political repercussions in the United States from this rising trade deficit could combine with specific trade disputes to have a negative impact on overall trade relations with some of the APEC countries such as China and Japan.

Figure 1 shows U.S. bilateral merchandise trade balances with the members of APEC. As can be seen, the largest deficits are with Japan, China, Canada, and Mexico, all important APEC members. Out of a total U.S. merchandise trade deficit of $436.5 billion in 2000, $285.2 billion was attributed to just seven APEC

---

[40] See CRS Report 98-928, *The World Trade Organization: Background and Issues*, by Lenore Sek.

[41] See CRS Report 97-291, *NAFTA: Related Environmental Issues and Initiatives*, by Mary Tiemann; and CRS Trade Electronic Briefing Book, *Labor Standards and Trade Agreements*, by Mary Jane Bolle, [http://www.congress.gov/brbk/html/ebtra25.html].

partner nations – five in Asia (China, Japan, Taiwan, Malaysia, and South Korea) plus two in North America (Canada and Mexico). The total U.S. trade imbalance with APEC reached $306.4 billion in 2000. Three-quarters of the imbalance in U.S. trade with the world, therefore, is with APEC. To the extent that the bilateral trade deficits with APEC countries are being exacerbated by trade barriers that are hindering access to their markets, trade liberalization under APEC may work to increase U.S. exports to those economies and reduce certain bilateral trade deficits. A lessening of a bilateral trade deficit through greater access to foreign markets, however, would tend to change the composition and distribution of the deficit and not necessarily reduce the overall deficit by a corresponding amount.

APEC also raises some fundamental questions for U.S. policy. One is whether a U.S. consensus can be achieved on the APEC vision of free trade and investment in the Asia Pacific region or whether future trade liberalization will be confined primarily to bilateral free-trade arrangements and multilateral trade negotiations under the WTO. Another question is whether the U.S. business community will continue to back the APEC process or whether they view the APEC goals of free trade and investment in the region as too long-term and too lofty to be actually achieved. A further question is whether trade promotion (fast-track) authority should be provided to the President that would cover negotiations under APEC. A final question is whether APEC is worth the effort and resources being devoted to it and whether the United States should continue to participate in it. These questions await a comprehensive domestic policy debate over APEC that is yet to occur.

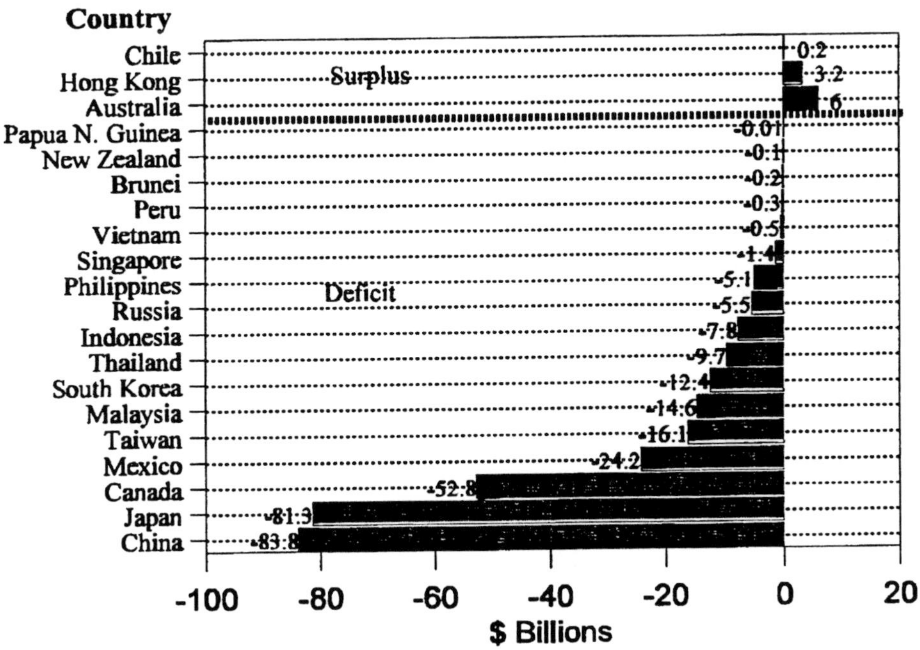

Figure 1. U.S. Merchandise Trade Balances with APEC Members 2000

Chapter 9

ASIA PACIFIC ECONOMIC COOPERATION (APEC), FREE TRADE, AND THE 2002 SUMMIT IN MEXICO[‡]

Dick K. Nanto

INTRODUCTION

The Asia Pacific Economic Cooperation (APEC) forum is an association of 21 economies bordering the Pacific Ocean who are working cooperatively to reduce barriers to trade and investment, facilitate the exchange of goods, services, resources, and technical know-how, and strengthen economic and technical cooperation. In 2000, APEC's 21 member economies had a combined Gross Domestic Product of over $19 trillion totaling about 48% of world exports. The members of APEC have declared their intention to establish free trade and investment in the region by the year 2010 for industrialized members and 2020 for the others. For the United States, APEC has become a key institution for pursuing trade and investment liberalization and facilitation in the Asia-Pacific region.

On October 26-27, 2002, the Tenth APEC Leaders' Meeting (summit) is to be hosted by Mexico in Las Cabos, Mexico. It is to be preceded by meetings of the senior officials from member nations, the APEC Business Advisory Council, and a CEO summit of business leaders. The APEC summit is usually attended by the

[‡] Excerpted from CRS Report RL31038. Updated October 17, 2002.

President, Secretary of State, U.S. Trade Representative, and Commerce Secretary. The official theme for APEC 2002 is to expand the benefits of cooperation for economic growth and development and enable the APEC vision to be implemented. APEC 2002 is intended to send a clear message to the world that APEC has the ability to implement its initiatives while responding and adapting to changes in the global and regional economies.

In September 2002, APEC Finance ministers agreed to adopt an action plan aimed at boosting efforts to block terrorist financing. The plan would increase the effectiveness of a freeze on terrorist-related assets by fully implementing current laws and working together in the arenas of law enforcement and information sharing.[1]

As in past Leader's meetings, Taiwan's President will not be allowed to attend because of objections by China. Taiwan has announced that it will send a delegation led by Nobel prize laureate Lee Yuan-tseh.

On October 20-21, 2001, the Ninth APEC Leaders' Meeting (summit) was held in Shanghai, China. President Bush, Secretary of State Powell, U.S. Trade Representative Zoellick, and other U.S. officials attended. The Leaders' Meeting was preceded by an APEC Ministerial Meeting on October 17-18 and by a series of other meetings during the year addressing various economic issues.

For 2001, China hosted the Leaders' Meeting and, in consultation with other APEC members, set the major agenda items. The official theme for 2001 was "Meeting New Challenges in the New Century: Achieving Common Prosperity through Participation and Cooperation" with sub-themes of: (1) sharing the benefits of globalization and the new economy, (2) advancing trade and investment, and (3) promoting sustained economic growth. The war on terrorism and slowing world economic growth, however, dominated discussions. The leaders' statement on counter-terrorism was the first time APEC dealt explicitly with a non-economic issue. In the statement, the leaders condemned the attacks on the United States, committed themselves to preventing and suppressing all forms of terrorists acts in the future, to enhance counter-terrorism cooperation, and take appropriate financial measures to prevent the flow of funds to terrorists.[2] APEC leaders also reaffirmed the goal of achieving free trade and investment among APEC members and strongly supported the launch of the new round of multilateral trade negotiations under the World Trade Organization.

At the Shanghai meeting, the leaders also issued the Shanghai Accord in

---

[1] Kosukegawa, Yoichi. APEC Agrees to Adopt Action Plan on Terrorist Financing. Japan Economic Newswire. September 5, 2002.

[2] Asia Pacific Economic Cooperation. APEC Leaders Statement on Counter-terrorism. Shanghai, China, October 21, 2001.

which they committed themselves to broaden APEC's vision for the future by identifying a conceptual and policy framework to guide APEC in the new century. The Accord included clarifying APEC's roadmap for achieving the free trade and investment goals on schedule with an assessment of overall progress in 2005, promoting the adoption of appropriate trade policies for the New Economy, following up on the APEC Trade Facilitation Principles, pursuing greater transparency in economic governance, and strengthening APEC's implementation mechanism.[3]

Representation by Taiwan at the Shanghai Leaders' Meeting became an issue when Beijing rejected Taiwan's choice of former Vice President Li Yuan-zu to attend. Beijing claimed that Mr. Li was not an economics official and consequently did not extend an official invitation to Taiwan to participate. The government of Taiwan refused to select another representative and ultimately boycotted the meeting.

APEC has become the primary regional institution in the Asia-Pacific for promoting open trade and practical economic cooperation. It is of interest to Congress because:

- it is becoming a vehicle for pursuing free trade and other initiatives similar in their longer-term objectives to the goals pursued under the North American Free Trade Agreement (NAFTA);
- the APEC Leaders' Meeting provides an opportunity for the U.S. President to raise and discuss issues with the heads of other APEC countries;
- any concrete trade or investment measures developed under APEC that require a change in existing U.S. laws will need legislative approval and may call for fast-track negotiating authority;
- the U.S. economy is linked to the economies of the Pacific rim through trade, financial investment, and direct investment in subsidiaries in the region; and
- in view of the intense debate over the effects of NAFTA, the proposed creation of a free-trade arrangement that includes the United States, China, Japan, South Korea, Taiwan, Indonesia, Russia, Vietnam, and other Asian-Pacific nations could easily become controversial.

---

[3] APEC. APEC Economic Leaders' Declaration, Shanghai, China. October 21, 2001.

The goal of establishing free trade and investment among APEC nations is being pursued along three tracks. The first is through liberalizing trade in certain sectors such as information technology. These have been referred to the World Trade Organization in order to bring European and other nations into the agreements and are categorized at the WTO as early voluntary sectoral liberalization (EVSL). The second is through bilateral free trade agreements or by encouraging multilateral trade negotiations under the WTO, and the third is through incremental liberalization measures (individual action plans) taken by APEC members.

In the 107th Congress, APEC is potentially affected by several legislative actions. Some trade liberalization under APEC arguably will require trade promotion (fast-track) negotiating authority (P.L. 107-210) and congressional approval. Several bills have been introduced that would authorize negotiations to establish free-trade areas with APEC countries. These include: S. 138 and S. 586 (with Chile) S.935 (with Australia), S. 943 (with New Zealand), S.944 (with the Republic of Korea), and H.R. 1566 (with Singapore, Australia, and New Zealand). H.Con.Res. 73 requested that during the 2001 APEC summit, the Presiden, call for the release of all Chinese political prisoners and Chinese ratification of the International Covenant on Civil and Political Rights. H.Con.Res. 194 called for APEC to allow participation by Taiwan's President Chen Shui-bian in the Shanghai Leader's Meeting. U.S. financial support for APEC falls under the State Department's budget (H.R. 1646/S. 1401) under Contributions to International Organizations and has been $601,000 per year.

Debate over trade liberalization under APEC also is likely to address whether provisions dealing with labor and the environment should be included and whether the United States would be able to respond to foreign country violations of labor or environmental standards with economic sanctions. U.S. participation in APEC also touches on the broader U.S. debate over whether the United States should continue to pursue the expansion of international trade and investment with other nations – particularly through free trade agreements, the effect of trade and globalization on import-sensitive industries, and whether increased trade threatens or enhances U.S. prosperity, employment opportunities, and economic security. The Bush Administration has been approached by leaders from many other nations who desire to pursue free trade agreements with the United States. USTR Zoellick stated that the Administration will consider each of these offers seriously, while focusing on the Free Trade Area of the Americas. By moving on multiple fronts, he stated that the United States could create a "competition in liberalization that will promote open markets in the Western hemisphere and around the world."[4] The Bush Administration also considers APEC to be important because of its role in promoting trade and investment liberalization, increased transparency, openness, and predictability based on the rule of law, and discussion among national leaders. The Administration also is working with the International Monetary Fund in fostering rapid Asian economic recovery which is thought to mean more exports for U.S. companies and more jobs for Americans.[5]

The growth of regional free-trade arrangements in various parts of the world also has generated proposals for other bilateral arrangements among APEC countries.[6] Free trade or preferential trade agreements have been announced or are under discussion among APEC members such as between Singapore and New Zealand, Australia, Japan, Mexico, Canada, and Chile and between Japan and South Korea. The ten countries of the Association of Southeast Asian Nations (ASEAN), Japan, China, and South Korea are considering an Asian free trade bloc (ASEAN + 3). Since 1992, the Association of Southeast Asian Nations (ASEAN) has been phasing in a Free Trade Area (AFTA) for its members, although AFTA's goal is currently to lower tariffs overall and eliminate them only on certain items imported from other member countries.

APEC Institutional Development

APEC began in 1989 as an Australian initiative in recognition of the growing interdependence among Asia-Pacific economies and in response to the free-trade areas which had developed in Europe and North America. Originally intended to exclude the United States and Canada, APEC was to provide an institution and forum for consultation and coordination on economic issues of importance to East Asia and Australia/New Zealand. Ultimately, membership was opened to countries in the Americas.

Membership in APEC initially included twelve economies (Hong Kong and Taiwan are not considered to be countries) but grew to twenty-one. The founding members were the United States, Canada, Japan, South Korea, ASEAN (Brunei, Indonesia, Malaysia, Philippines, Singapore, and Thailand, but not Vietnam), Australia, and New Zealand. In 1991, the People's Republic of China, Taiwan, and Hong Kong joined. In 1993, Mexico and Papua New Guinea were admitted,

---

[4] Zoellick, Robert B. "Free Trade and the Hemispheric Hope." Prepared Remarks of Robert B. Zoellick, U.S. Trade Representative, Council of the Americas, Washington, D.C., May 7, 2001.

[5] U.S. Department of State. Bureau of East Asian and Pacific Affairs. Why APEC Matters to Americans. Fact Sheet, February 28, 2001.

[6] Currently, over 130 regional trade agreements are in force. Most provide for reduced trade barriers rather than free trade. Since 1995, the WTO received notifications of 90 agreements.

as was Chile in 1994. In 1997, APEC extended membership to Peru, Russia, and Vietnam (who became members in 1998) and declared a ten-year period of consolidation before additional membership applications would be considered.

The objectives of APEC are:

- to sustain growth and development of the region;
- to encourage the flow of goods, services, capital, and technology;
- to develop and strengthen the multilateral trading system; and
- to reduce barriers to trade in goods and services and investment.

APEC's principles of operation are:

- that APEC is a voluntary association in which participants do not cede powers of regulation or enforcement to a supra-national institution;
- that decisions are based on consensus; and
- that decisions are implemented by individual members on a voluntary basis and by collective actions (the voluntary actions are coordinated and aimed at accomplishing a common goal).

At the 1994 summit in Bogor, Indonesia, APEC leaders signed a declaration setting the goal of free and open trade and investment in APEC. The industrialized economies (United States, Japan, Canada, Australia, New Zealand, Singapore, and possibly others) are to achieve the goal by the year 2010 and the remaining economies to do so by 2020. The United States argued against allowing the additional 10 years for developing economies, but this provision was retained primarily at the insistence of China, South Korea, and Malaysia. The Bogor Declaration is a consensus, not a legal, document.

THE APEC STRUCTURE AND ACTIVITIES

The APEC chair rotates annually and since 1989 has been held by Australia, Singapore, South Korea, Thailand, United States, Indonesia, Japan, the Philippines, Canada, Malaysia, New Zealand, and Brunei. China holds the chair in 2001.

The focal point of APEC activities is the annual **Leaders Meeting** in which the APEC leaders set goals, publicize them, and provide momentum for the process.[7] This is usually held in November of each year, and is attended by heads of state except for those from Taiwan (Chinese Taipei) and Hong Kong who send other representatives. The major APEC decisions are affirmed and announced at this meeting. The summit also provides a platform for and gives momentum to major APEC initiatives. The Leaders' meeting was begun in 1993 by former President Clinton who invited the leaders to Blake Island near Seattle. Although APEC confines its agenda to economic issues, the heads of state at bilateral meetings conducted before and after the Leader's Meetings have discussed concerns over international security, human rights, and other issues.

Most of the decisions of APEC are first considered in **ministerial meetings**. These include the respective ministers dealing with trade, finance, transportation, telecommunications, human resources development (education), energy, environment, science and technology, and small and medium-sized enterprises. The largest ministerial is the annual **Joint Ministerial Meeting** which precedes the Leaders Meeting. It usually is attended by foreign and trade or commerce ministers from member states. Management of substance is handled under ministerial direction through **Senior Officials Meetings** (held four times per year). In 1993, APEC created a **Secretariat** in Singapore with an Executive Director, 23 officials seconded by member economies for fixed terms and a similar number of locally recruited support staff.

Most of the specific tasks before APEC are being addressed in **committees or working groups** or expert groups that deal with economic issues of importance to the region. For implementing the Bogor declaration, the Committee on Trade and Investment plays the key role. Other committees are the Economic Committee and the Budget and Administrative Committee. APEC also has ten working groups which work on specific areas of cooperation and facilitation: (1) Trade and Investment Data, (2) Trade Promotion, (3) Industrial Science and Technology, (4) Human Resources Development, (5) Energy Cooperation, (6) Marine Resource Conservation, (7) Telecommunications, (8) Transportation, (9) Tourism, and (10) Fisheries. Each working group has one or more shepherds (members) who take responsibility for coordinating the work of the group.

In 1992, APEC formed the **Eminent Persons Group** (EPG) and charged it with developing a "vision" for APEC's future. In 1994, the EPG recommended that APEC establish the goal of free trade, and, in 1995, as it completed its work, it recommended ways to achieve that vision.

In 1995, APEC established the **APEC Business Advisory Council** (ABAC)

[7] Bergsten, C. Fred, ed. *Whither APEC?* Washington, Institute for International Economics, 1997. pp. 3-4. Note: The Leaders Meetings are technically not summits because of Hong Kong and Taiwan whose leaders are not officially heads of state.

which consists of up to three members appointed by each APEC member. It provides advice on implementing the APEC agenda and other specific business-related issues.[8] For 2000, ABAC focused its activities on maintaining momentum in trade and investment liberalization, building capacity in APEC financial systems, and improving access to new opportunities through technological progress. In 2001, ABAC is expanding the work of its Action Plan Monitoring Committee and developing recommendations from three task forces dealing, respectively, with finance, technology, and trade and investment.

In 1995, the issue was raised of whether APEC should be expanded to include consideration of regional security issues. Until then, consideration of non-economic issues was confined to bilateral summit meetings surrounding the Leaders Meetings. APEC had carefully kept its distance from security matters for fear that such issues would cause divisions within the group — particularly among China, Taiwan, the United States, Japan, and Russia. Such divisions could thwart cooperation in achieving economic goals. The consensus in 1995 among APEC members seemed to be that regional security issues should be discussed in the ASEAN Regional Forum and other fora rather than in APEC.[9] The ASEAN Regional Forum usually meets after the ASEAN Ministerial Conference and, in addition to the seven members of ASEAN, includes the United States, China, Russia, Japan, South Korea, Australia, New Zealand, Canada, and the European Union. It provides the largest pan-Pacific forum for discussing security issues.

THE 1995 OSAKA ACTION AGENDA

Before 1995, APEC declarations and other documents were general statements without specifics on measures to be taken. In 1995 at the meetings in Osaka, Japan, APEC members agreed to an Action Agenda that was intended to translate into reality the aims of APEC) particularly the 1994 Bogor Declaration of achieving free trade and investment among its member economies by the year 2010 or 2020.[10]

The Osaka Action Agenda is the template adopted for APEC work to accomplish its three goals of: (1) trade and investment liberalization, (2) trade and investment facilitation, and (3) economic and technical cooperation. The Agenda

---

[8] U.S. representatives to ABAC are: Ernest Micek, Chairman of Cargill, Paul Y. Song, CEO of the ARIS Corporation, and Seymour Sternberg, Chairman and CEO of New York Life.

[9] Moosa, Eugene. *Regional Security Remains a Taboo at APEC*. Reuters Newswire Service. November 19, 1995.

[10] Asia Pacific Economic Cooperation. *The Osaka Action Agenda*. November 19, 1995.

laid out nine general principles for members to follow in devising a road map to reach APEC's free-trade goal. These general principles have been used to guide individual APEC members in devising national Action Plans for submission at subsequent meetings.

The **general principles** in the Action Plan included (1) comprehensiveness [all impediments are to be included], (2) WTO-consistency [consistent with World Trade Organization rules], (3) comparability [comparable actions with consideration for different starting points], (4) non-discrimination [benefits to be accorded to all APEC members and also to non-APEC countries], (5) transparency [in domestic trade laws and regulations], (6) standstill [no increased protection], (7) simultaneous start continuous process-differentiated time tables [all start together in a continuous process to achieve long-term goal], (8) flexibility [in dealing with issues arising from liberalization] a controversial principle that some argue allows for import-sensitive sectors to be liberalized more slowly], and (9) cooperation [to pursue economic and technical cooperation].

The Agenda also outlined actions that APEC economies were to take in fifteen specific areas. These included both actions by individual members and collectively by APEC in tariffs, non-tariff measures, services, investment, standards, customs procedures, intellectual property rights, competition policy, and dispute mediation.

Each APEC member also announced **initial actions** for liberalization and facilitation of trade and investment. These actions represented the first wide-ranging initiatives of APEC members to speed up implementing their Uruguay Round commitments.

Since Japan hosted the 1995 APEC meetings in Osaka, it held the Chair and the responsibility to ensure that the APEC process of trade and investment liberalization continued. Japan, however, took this opportunity to lead a group (including South Korea, China, and Taiwan) of members who argued for a weak definition of comprehensiveness[11] and insisted on including a general **principle of flexibility** that might allow the country to placate certain import-sensitive sectors (particularly agriculture) by putting them on a slower timetable or possibly even excluding them from complete liberalization. The United States and twelve APEC members viewed the principle of comprehensiveness (coverage of all sectors) as

[11] October 25, 1995, Representatives Doug Bereuter and Howard L. Berman along with 27 other Members of the U.S. House of Representatives sent a letter to Secretary of State Warren Christopher and USTR Mickey Kantor urging the Clinton Administration not to weaken its resolve to press for "the promised comprehensive and detailed agenda for implementing the Bogor Declaration."

vital to achieving the Bogor vision of free trade in APEC. In Osaka, APEC members reached a compromise that allowed the comprehensiveness principle to remain unchanged but added the principle of flexibility.[12]

At Osaka, Malaysia also argued for making all APEC commitments "voluntary" (meaning that the free-trade target dates would not be binding). For the Bogor Declaration in 1994, Malaysia had attached its objections to establishing the goal of free trade and investment by the year 2010 or 2020. As a compromise, the word "voluntary" was added. The Osaka Leaders' Declaration stated APEC's resolve to "encourage...the evolving efforts of **voluntary liberalization** in the region," but the Osaka Action Agenda clearly declared under the comprehensiveness principle that "the APEC liberalization and facilitation process will be comprehensive, addressing all impediments to achieving the long-term goal of free and open trade and investment."[13]

APEC members also disagreed over the **non-discrimination principle** or what has been termed "open regionalism." Japan has pressed for the benefits of APEC trade liberalization to be accorded even non-APEC trading partners on a mostfavored- nation basis. Japan's government had stated that it thought APEC should not be a trading bloc that discriminates against outsiders. The problem with such unilateral trade liberalization, however, is that it invites free riders and makes generating public support difficult. The United States favored benefits to be accorded non-APEC countries on a reciprocal basis which has been the basis for other negotiations.[14] In practice, APEC agreements have gone to the WTO for binding and global implementation with non-APEC members.

THE 1996 MANILA ACTION PLAN

For the APEC Leaders' Meeting in the Philippines in November 1996, the theme was "from vision to action" meaning that APEC members were taking measures to realize the goal of free and open trade and investment in the region. The APEC leaders:

- launched the implementation phase of the free and open trade and

---

[12] The flexibility principle reads: Considering the different levels of economic development among the APEC economies and the diverse circumstances in each economy, flexibility will be available in dealing with issues arising from such circumstances in the liberalization and facilitation process.

[13] APEC. *Osaka Action Agenda*, p. 1.

[14] Johnstone, Christopher B. *An Awkward Dance: The Osaka Summit, Japanese Leadership and the Future of APEC.* JEI Report, October 20, 1995. p. 12.

investment agenda,
- delivered business facilitation measures,
- agreed to advance common goals in the World Trade Organization,
- developed ways to strengthen economic and technical cooperation, and
- engaged the business sector as a full partner in the APEC process.[15]

In concrete terms, the first task was to coordinate the individual and collective initiatives into a Manila Action Plan for APEC. This contained the first steps of an evolutionary process of progressive and comprehensive trade and investment liberalization toward achieving the goals in the Bogor Declaration and in accord with the Osaka Action Agenda.

APEC took each of the Individual Action Plans (IAP) by member economies and categorized them according to the fifteen issue areas set forth in the Osaka Action Plan. Although the APEC process relies on concerted unilateral liberalization and does not formally evaluate each IAP, there was considerable pressure placed on countries whose plans fell short. One of the principles of the process is comparability — which means no free riding.

The APEC leaders also announced that APEC supported an Information Technology Agreement (ITA) that was then passed on to the WTO for global consideration and broader support. The agreement grew out of recommendations from industry groups in 1995 to the Group of Seven (G-7) industrialized nations. It was endorsed by U.S. and European corporate executives at a November 1995 Transatlantic Business Dialogue, further endorsed by the United States and European Union at the Madrid Summit in December 1995, and then supported by the Quadrilateral (U.S., EU, Canada, and Japan) Trade Ministers and the G-7 in 1996 before APEC decided to support it in November 1996. By the time it was considered (and adopted) by the WTO in December 1996, 14 states or customs territories were prepared to sign the agreement. The ITA provides for zero tariffs in more than 92% of information technology trade among its 39 signatory nations. The tariff reductions were phased in over the 1997-2000 period, although developing country participants have been granted extended periods for some products.[16] APEC played a key role in generating support for this initiative among the newly industrializing Asia-Pacific nations.

---

[15] APEC. *APEC Economic Leaders' Declaration: From Vision to Action*. November 25, 1996.

[16] See the Information Technology Agreement on the WTO website at [http://www.wto.org/wto/english/tratop_e/inftec_e/inftec_e.htm].

THE 1997 VANCOUVER MEETINGS – THE MANILA FRAMEWORK

The 1997 Ministerial and Leaders Meetings took place in November in Vancouver, British Columbia. As the leaders met, several of the Asian APEC members were coping with severe financial crises in which the value of their currencies had plummeted, the value of stocks on their equity markets had dropped, and many of their financial institutions had become insolvent.[17] The International Monetary Fund had already arranged support packages for Thailand and Indonesia and was in the process of doing the same for South Korea.

While the APEC professionals considered the Asian financial crisis a diversion from the APEC agenda for trade and investment liberalization, it added a dimension to a Leaders Meeting that would otherwise have been a rather humdrum event. Prior to the summit, the APEC finance ministers had met in Manila and developed a framework to deal with currency and other financial crises. The ministers rejected a Japanese-backed proposal to establish a separate Asian fund to provide financial support for countries coping with financial difficulties. The Manila Framework was endorsed by the APEC leaders.

The Manila framework included three elements. The first was a strong domestic response by each country involved to create an economic environment that can attract capital and maintain confidence] including to strengthen its banking system. The second was a stronger response by the IMF that included adequate financial support up front to ease any liquidity crisis and to provide the confidence necessary to avoid instability. The third was a cooperative financing mechanism through which the countries of the region would, on a case-by-case basis, backstop IMF financial measures to ensure that adequate resources were available.[18]

At the APEC summit, the leaders also designated fifteen major sectors where the principal goal would be to achieve free trade (tariff elimination) within a short span of years but not later than the year 2005. This represented a restricted, but nevertheless significant, advance on the Bogor Declaration. Detailed market-opening plans were to be concluded by the first half of 1998 with the aim of beginning implementation in 1999. These Early Voluntary Sectoral Liberalization (EVSL) agreements would be patterned after the Information Technology Agreement endorsed in 1996 at the Manila summit and later adopted by the WTO.

---

[17] See CRS Report RL30272, *Global Financial Turmoil, the IMF, and the New Financial Architecture*, by Dick K. Nanto.

[18] Summers, Larry. Press Briefing, Vancouver, BC. November 24, 1997.

Of the fifteen sectors, nine were chosen for action. Of these nine, six had been nominated by the United States. The nine sectors were: environmental goods and services, energy sector, fish and fish products, toys, forest products, gems and jewelry, medical equipment and instruments, chemicals, and a telecommunications mutual recognition arrangement.[19]

Although these EVSL initiatives were begun by APEC, APEC members agreed to send them to the WTO in order to seek participation by the EU and other nations and to make the commitments binding. At the WTO, except for the telecommunications mutual recognition arrangement, the liberalization of these sectors has became entangled in the proposal for a new round of trade negotiations, and progress has stalled.

Each APEC member also submitted a 1997 Individual Action Plan that indicated measures taken and outlined how it intended to move toward the Bogor targets. Another area of focus for the 1997 APEC meetings was trade facilitation and other measures to lower the costs of doing business in the region. The ministers welcomed the achievements under what are called Collective Action Plans that lower costs and reduce barriers to the movement of goods and services, capital, and business people. They endorsed work in these areas, which included: development of the Blueprint for Customs Modernization; establishment of APEC Internet sites; progress on alignment with international standards; increased transparency for acquiring and using intellectual property rights; development of options to enhance the environment for investment; development of model mutual recognition agreements; principles to guide work on dispute mediation; improved mobility for business people (including the APEC Business Travel Card); providing Internet access to member country tariff rates; and development of guidelines for improving the tendering, approval, and regulatory processes for independent power producers.[20]

THE 1998 MALAYSIA MEETINGS – SECTORAL LIBERALIZATION

The 1998 APEC Joint Ministerial and Leaders' Meetings were held in Kuala Lumpur, Malaysia. Former President Clinton had announced his intention to attend, but sent Vice President Gore in his place because of the imminent

[19] APEC. *APEC Ministers on Early Sectoral Liberalization* (Annex to APEC Ministers Joint Statement).

[20] APEC. *Asia-Pacific Economic Cooperation (APEC) Ninth Ministerial Meeting Joint Statement.* Available on the World Wide Web at [http://www.apecsec.org.sg].

bombing of Iraq. At the Malaysia meetings, APEC leaders gave support to Early Voluntary Sectoral Liberalization (EVSL) at the WTO which would liberalize trade in nine key sectors as APEC had proposed in the previous Leader's Meeting.[21]

Two other issues dominated the APEC meetings in Malaysia. The first was the global economic turmoil that began in Asia in 1997. APEC Leaders declared that they needed to deal urgently with the financial crisis and committed themselves to pursuing a cooperative growth strategy with the following dimensions:

- Growth-oriented prudent macroeconomic policies, appropriate to the specific requirements of each of their economies;
- Expanded financial assistance from the international community to generate employment and to build and strengthen social safety nets to protect the poor and vulnerable;
- A comprehensive program of support for efforts to strengthen financial systems, restore trade finance, and accelerate corporate sector restructuring;
- New approaches to catalyze the return of stable and sustainable private capital flows into the region;
- A renewed commitment to the Bogor goals of achieving free and open trade and investment within APEC; and
- Looking toward the longer-term, urgent work among themselves and with other economies and institutions to develop and implement measures to strengthen the international financial system.[22]

Prior to the APEC meetings, Japan had been urged by the United States and other industrialized nations to stimulate its economy in order to restore domestic demand-led growth, clean up its banking system, further open its markets, deregulate its economy, and do more to help its neighboring countries in crisis. In the weeks leading up to the APEC Leaders' Meeting, Japan did take three measures aimed at restoring its moribund economy and promoting growth in east Asian countries. It announced a stimulus package (its eighth in the 1990s) of

---

[21] Office of the United States Trade Representative. *APEC Telecommunications Equipment Mutual Recognition Arrangement*. Press Release 98 - 58. June 5, 1998. On Internet at [http://www.ustr.gov/releases/1998/06/index.html].

[22] APEC. *1998 APEC Economic Leaders' Declaration*. On Internet at [http://www.usia.gov/admin/025/wwwhkld.html].

public spending and tax cuts worth about $196 billion,[23] unveiled what it called the Miyazawa Initiative — a package of support measures by the Japanese government totaling $30 billion to assist economic recovery in Asian countries,[24] and, jointly with the United States, announced a new $10 billion multilateral initiative aimed at revitalizing private sector growth in Asia.[25]

Another issue had high visibility at the meetings in Malaysia. Malaysian Prime Minister Mahathir Mohamad, who hosted the APEC meetings, had been a severe critic of the APEC trade liberalization process. As the Asian financial crisis battered the Malaysian economy, Mahathir imposed currency controls and restrictions on capital flows to and from Malaysia and stifled dissent within the country.[26] The capital restrictions were in conflict with the goal of free trade and investment in APEC but had attracted sympathy from other nations that had suffered the flight of short-term capital. Mahathir also had his former Deputy Prime Minister Anwar Ibrahim (who had opposed Mahathir and certain of his policies) arrested on a "morals charge." In October 1998, Reps. Ben Gilman and Doug Bereuter urged President Clinton to seek a new venue for the November APEC summit because his attendance in Malaysia might be perceived as an endorsement of the "anti-free market measures" put in place by that country and as a signal that the United States approved of the arrest of Anwar Ibrahim.[27] At the APEC summit, no bilateral meetings had been scheduled between President Clinton and Prime Minister Mahathir, and Clinton's non-attendance because of Iraq had an additional muting effect. While in Malaysia for the Joint Ministerial Meeting, then Secretary of State Albright met with the wife of the jailed former Deputy Prime Minister, and in a speech at a banquet hosted by Prime Minister Mahathir, then Vice President Gore voiced sympathy for Malaysia's pro-democracy forces. Both of these actions brought strong negative reactions from Malaysian officials.[28]

---

[23] Sugawara, Sandra. "Japanese Set Plan for Economy." *Washington Post*, November 16, 1998. P. A21. Japan. Economic Planning Agency. *Outline of Emergency Economic Package*. On Internet at [http://www.epa.go.jp/98/b/19981116b-taisaku-e.html].

[24] Japan. Ministry of Finance. *New Initiative to Overcome the Asian Currency Crisis*. October 3, 1998. On Internet at [http://www.mof.go.jp/english/daijin/e1e042.htm].

[25] The White House. Joint Statement by President Clinton and Prime Minister Obuchi. November 16, 1998. On Internet at [http://library.whitehouse.gov].

[26] For a summary of the controls, see Aziz, Zeti Akhtar. *Preparing for the New International Financial Architecture: Malaysia's Programme*. Speech at the International Conference on "Managing the Asian Financial Crisis: Lessons & Challenges" on November 2-3, 1998. On Internet at [http://www.bnm.gov.my/spch/1998/1102.htm].

[27] "Gilman, Bereuter Urge Clinton to Boycott APEC Summit in Malaysia." *Inside U.S. Trade*, October 30, 1998. Internet edition at [http://www.insidetrade.com].

[28] Blustein, Paul. "Gore Remarks Anger Malaysian Leaders." *Washington Post*. November 17, 1998. P. A29.

The 1999 New Zealand Summit – End of Financial Crisis

On September 12-13, 1999, the Seventh APEC Leaders Meeting was held in Auckland, New Zealand. The 1999 APEC meetings occurred earlier than their usual time because the World Trade Organization's Ministerial Conference was to be held in Seattle on November 30-December 3, 1999. APEC wanted to complete its recommendations for the WTO with enough time for them to be considered for the WTO Conference. The APEC leaders endorsed the launching of a new WTO round of multilateral trade negotiations and agreed that the new round of trade negotiations should: (1) include industrial tariffs as well as mandated negotiations on services and agriculture, (2) lead to timely and effective improvements in market access to the benefit of all participants, particularly developing countries, (3) have a balanced and sufficiently broad-based agenda, and (4) be concluded within three years as a single package but which would not preclude the possibility of early results on a provisional basis. For the new WTO round, the APEC leaders also: (5) supported the abolition of agricultural export subsidies and unjustifiable export restrictions, (6) agreed that the current moratorium on duties on electronic commerce should be extended, and (7) endorsed efforts to achieve an agreement on transparency in government procurement. The leaders also agreed to continue working on the remaining eight sectors designated for accelerated tariff liberalization (EVSL) in the WTO with the goal (not attained) of completed agreements in 1999.[29]

The problem of Japan's protection of its rice farmers arose at APEC 99. Japan and some other APEC members insisted that APEC support the position in the WTO trade negotiations that the agreements for all sectors be concluded in one package rather than have separate sectoral agreements implemented after they were concluded. The United States preferred separate sectoral agreements in order that the eight sectors designated for early voluntary sectoral liberalization by APEC in 1998 and other action on freeing trade in certain sectors could go forward without waiting for the end of the WTO trade round. Japan, however, was under pressure from its farmers not to open its rice market. It reportedly felt that the more products that were covered by the negotiations, the less attention would

[29] APEC Secretariat. Leaders' Declaration - New Zealand. Press Release 47/99, September 13, 1999. On Internet at [http://www.apecsec.org.sg]. U.S. Trade Representative. Statement of United States Trade Representative Charlene Barshefsky at the Conclusion of the APEC Ministerial Sessions in Auckland, New Zealand. Press Release 99-73, September 10, 1999.

be drawn to its high rice import tariffs.[30] Also, by not allowing agreements in sectors to go forward before the conclusion of the round, proponents of the "single package" theory reportedly felt that there would be less chance that an agreement on agriculture could be concluded early.

The APEC summit occurred at a time of increasing violence in East Timor following its vote for independence from Indonesia. APEC leaders took advantage of bilateral meetings with each other to put pressure on Indonesia to allow international peacekeepers into the country. While APEC was in session, Indonesian President Habibie bowed to international concerns and agreed to allow a United Nations peacekeeping force into East Timor.[31]

The APEC summit also occurred when the Asian economies appeared to be recovering from the economic crisis that had beset the region and certain other nations of the world since July 1997. As Thailand, Indonesia, the Philippines, South Korea, Japan, Hong Kong, and other Asian countries dropped into recession, their enthusiasm for further opening of their markets had waned. However, with the exception of Indonesia, the APEC economies seemed to have turned the corner, and there was heightened recognition that open, transparent, and well-governed markets were key to a return to sustained economic growth and prosperity. The general assessment of APEC's ability to cope with the Asian financial crisis, however, seemed to be that APEC really did little substantive work and that the International Monetary Fund, World Bank, the U.S. Treasury, and other players in international financial markets carried the burden of coping with the crisis.[32] In order to bring APEC finance ministers more into the mainstream of APEC activities, the finance ministerial meeting was moved to the period immediately preceding the Leaders meeting.

At New Zealand, the meeting between President Clinton and China's President Jiang, Zemin gave impetus to talks on China's accession to the WTO which had been suspended following the bombing of the Chinese embassy in Belgrade, Yugoslavia. The two also discussed Taiwan's alleged "pro-independence gambit" and North Korea and human rights issues.[33]

---

[30] Shimizu, Yasumasa. "Rich Issue Again Raising Global Hackles." *Nikkei Weekly*, August 30, 1999. p. 3.

[31] Richburg, Keith B. "Jakarta Asks U.N. Force to End E. Timor Turmoil." *Washington Post*, September 13, 1999. p. 1A.

[32] See, for example, Sanger, David E. "Some Birthday Cake for a Toothless Wonder." *New York Times*, September 12, 1999.

[33] China's leaders have expressed concern over Taiwan President Lee Teng-hui's statement in July 1999 that Taiwan-China ties should be conducted on a "state-to-state" basis. See: Lam, Willy Wo-Lap, "Jiang to Pressure Clinton over Taiwan Stance." South China Morning Post. August 14, 1999. U.S. Information Agency. The White House at Work, President Clinton: Key Achievements from the APEC Summit, September 16, 1999.

THE 2000 BRUNEI SUMMIT – TOWARD BILATERAL FTAS

On November 15-16, 2000, the Eighth APEC Leaders' Meeting was held in Bandar Seri Begawan, Brunei. During the bilateral meeting with Singapore, the United States and Singapore announced that they would begin negotiations on a bilateral free trade agreement.[34] Given the stalled start of the WTO multilateral negotiations, more and more countries were opting to proceed with bilateral free trade agreements. During other bilateral meetings, the United States, New Zealand, Singapore, Brunei, and Chile agreed in principle to an "open skies" pact (eliminating restrictions on airline flights, prices, and routes among themselves),[35] and the U.S. and China announced that China would ban certain missile-related exports in exchange for a lifting of U.S. sanctions prohibiting Chinese launches of American satellites.[36]

In the Brunei summit, the APEC leaders reaffirmed their determination to realize the goal of free and open trade and investment among member economies and agreed on the need to expeditiously launch a new round of trade negotiations under the World Trade Organization in 2001. In a concession to developing country members (particularly Malaysia), the leaders called for a balanced and sufficiently broad-based agenda that would respond to the interests and concerns of all WTO members to be finalized as soon as possible in 2001. The APEC communique also stated that China should be accepted into the WTO soon, followed by Taiwan and sometime later by Russia and Vietnam; that the people in every economy should have access to information and services offered via the Internet by 2010; and that countries recovering from the 1997-98 Asian financial crisis should keep up with painful economic reforms even though their economies now are recovering.[37]

POLICY ASSESSMENT AND IMPLICATIONS

Trade liberalization under APEC is nowhere near as far along as that under either the European Union or the North America Free Trade Agreement. APEC's

---

[34] See CRS Report RS20755, *Singapore-U.S. Free Trade Agreement*, by Dick K. Nanto

[35] U.S. Department of Transportation. United States, Asia-Pacific Aviation Partners Enter Multilateral Open Skies Agreement. DOT Press Release 222-00, November 15, 2000.

[36] Perlez, Jane. China to Stop Selling A-Arms Delivery Systems. *New York Times*, November 21, 2000. P. A12.

[37] APEC Secretariat. Delivering to the Community, APEC Economic Leaders' Declaration, Bandar Seri Begawan, Brueni Darussalam. November 16, 2000. On Internet at [http://www.apecsec.org.sg].

goal of free trade is to be phased in over the next two decades. Only the framework now exists to lead APEC members toward that goal. APEC is not a negotiating body nor are its decisions legally binding on its members. The APEC process has been called "concerted unilateral action" in which a set of principles and guidelines are agreed to by APEC members and used to steer individual member actions. Rather than a trade bloc, APEC can be characterized as a building block toward greater trade liberalization and cooperation not only within the organization, itself, but in broader contexts, such as in the World Trade Organization. The APEC work programs are conducted on the basis of open dialogue with equal respect for the views of all participants – both the member countries and, to a certain extent, private business interests. This consensus-based decision making, however, tends to be slow and cumbersome.

When APEC began, many thought it would be just another "talk shop." The movement in APEC toward voluntary free trade and investment liberalization, however, has gone beyond initial expectations and seems to reflect a change in world economic circumstances and attitudes. The nations belonging to the WTO already have agreed to reduce tariffs and eliminate most non-tariff barriers. For the industrialized nations, in particular, tariffs already are so low in many sectors that some argue that dropping them entirely would make little difference. Until the onset of the Asian financial crisis in 1997, many nations were discovering the advantages of free trade and unfettered foreign investment in today's fast moving, consumer-oriented markets. A perception was developing that closed markets and unfriendly investment climates can cause economies to lose rather than create employment opportunities. Since the 1997-99 Asian financial crisis and ensuing slow down in economic growth, however, some nations are taking a second look at the costs as well as advantages of free trade and capital flows — particularly short-term capital flows between wealthy and developing economies.

In terms of U.S. interests, APEC promotes trade and cooperation among economies that have been the most dynamic in the world, encourages open trading systems rather than trading blocs, helps U.S. businesses remain engaged in the region, and provides the Asia-Pacific region with a counterweight to the European Union. In response to APEC, the European Union in 1996 initiated ASEM, the Asia- Europe Meeting, which excludes the Americas.[38] At the same time,

[38] ASEM met for the first time, on March 1-2, 1996, in Bangkok, Thailand. It included Heads of State and Government of ten Asian Nations (ASEAN plus China, Japan, and Korea) and fourteen members of the European Union plus the European Commission. The initial purpose has been to allow the leaders to become better acquainted with each other in order to build a foundation for further and continued cooperation among the participating countries. For information on U.S.-EU trade, see CRS Report 97-734, *The Transatlantic Business Dialogue*, by Glennon Harrison.

countries in the Americas are pursuing the Free Trade Area of the Americas (FTAA) a free-trade arrangement that would stretch from Canada to Chile.[39]

Critics of APEC include those who (1) assert that liberalized trade and investment has been primarily a one-way street that benefits trading partners more than the United States; (2) are concerned that the U.S. President should not be meeting annually with the heads of state of countries with alleged human rights problems (for example, China, Indonesia, and Vietnam), and (3) place higher priority on environmental considerations than trade.

Some import sensitive sectors also have opposed further opening of U.S. markets and more free trade agreements. They fear that APEC free trade could become a two-edged sword. U.S. firms could gain greater access to Asian and South American markets, but exporters from those regions also would gain more access to U.S. markets. There are concerns that this could hurt previously protected American industries, such as apparel, agriculture, steel, and motor vehicles (notably, pickup trucks). Some in these import-sensitive industries have opposed liberalized imports from Asia and Latin America. Also, in light of the intense opposition from some in the United States concerning granting China the trade privileges of normal-trade-relations (most-favored-nation) status and allowing it to join the World Trade Organization, the question remains of how Americans would respond to establishing free trade with that nation. Furthermore, given the hidden barriers to trade and investment in countries like Japan (close business relationships, interlocking corporate organizations, etc.), some have questioned whether free trade with Japan might be a one-way street. Would Japanese exporters gain unlimited access to the U.S. market, while American exporters still would face a web of private trade barriers in Japan?

APEC is maturing as an organization and has now drawn most major players in the Asia-Pacific region into its membership. Its long-range goals are lofty, but it seems to be moving steadily toward achieving them. It is becoming a credible vehicle to discuss and coordinate issues in the region as well as to achieve trade and investment liberalization. The Asian financial crisis dampened enthusiasm for further opening of markets, but the crisis also underlined the need for market discipline in allocating financial resources. Market discipline occurs partly through liberalized trade and capital flows.

The Individual Action Plans that are to bring the member economies closer to the APEC goal of free trade and investment in the region contain many significant actions. Most tariff reductions, however, reflect what member governments

[39] See CRS Report RS20864, *A Free Trade Area of the Americas: Status of Negotiations and Major Policy Issues*, by J. F. Hornbeck.

already are committed to do in the World Trade Organization. Some regulations have been changed in response to APEC efforts, but for most countries, only a few actions to reduce tariffs or ease foreign investment requirements have been taken specifically to achieve the APEC goals. The time has arrived, however, when APEC members will have to consider concrete measures that go beyond those already scheduled in order to achieve the goals of the Bogor Declaration.

The sectors designated for early voluntary trade liberalization at the 1998 APEC summit have been one way of going beyond the WTO commitments, although this sectoral liberalization effort has been stalled at the WTO. Another strategy that has been suggested would be to adopt the APEC goals of free trade by the year 2010 or 2020 as a goal for the next round of multilateral trade negotiations under the WTO. This would put the rest of the WTO members on the same timetable as those in APEC. If the WTO members were to adopt this APEC goal, many of the problems now being debated within APEC would be solved. This includes the question of whether APEC trade and investment liberalization also would apply to non-APEC nations and whether APEC is to become an exclusive trading bloc.[40] The WTO, however, includes more countries than does APEC. This makes reaching a consensus to pursue such a goal more difficult and more unlikely to be to be achieved quickly. The WTO also is attempting to pursue its own agenda for future negotiations.[41]

Another strategy that countries are pursuing to go beyond their WTO obligations is to negotiate free-trade agreements with other APEC members. In view of the difficulty in launching a new round of multilateral trade negotiations under the WTO and the slow progress under APEC, many individual members are electing to go down the route of bilateral free trade agreements.

On the other hand, within the United States, those who question the expansion of international trade and investment often argue that the U.S. should not pursue more free-trade arrangements because of human rights, economic, and other concerns. Import-sensitive industries are among those who often oppose granting other nations greater access to U.S. markets. They also are less interested in access to foreign markets that might be accorded through trade and investment liberalization. Controversy also continues over the extent to which environmental and labor conditions should be included in such agreements.[42] Anti-globalization

---

[40] Bergsten, C. Fred. "APEC in 1997: Prospects and Possible Strategies." In C. Fred Bergsten, Ed. *Whither APEC?* Washington, Institute for International Economics, 1997. p. 6.

[41] See CRS Report 98-928, *The World Trade Organization: Background and Issues*, by Lenore Sek.

[42] See CRS Report 97-291, *NAFTA: Related Environmental Issues and Initiatives*, by Mary Tiemann; and CRS Trade Electronic Briefing Book, *Labor Standards and Trade Agreements*, by Mary Jane Bolle, [http://www.congress.gov/brbk/html/ebtra25.html].

protesters who have directed their efforts mainly to oppose WTO, International Monetary Fund, and World Bank activities also could oppose further trade liberalization under APEC.

APEC is also facing the growing pains of any new organization. Some of its committees and working groups have overlapping interests. The number of meetings is increasing, and travel requirements are rising for participants. Still, it has, so far, avoided forming a large bureaucracy such as those in the Organization for Economic Cooperation and Development or the European Union. Also, it has expanded its scope to address financial problems as well as trade and investment.

For the United States, a problem related to APEC is that the U.S. merchandise trade balance with the APEC member economies has been deteriorating. This can be attributed mostly to U.S. macroeconomic conditions, but the political repercussions in the United States from this rising trade deficit could combine with specific trade disputes to have a negative impact on overall trade relations with some of the APEC countries such as China and Japan.

Figure 1 shows U.S. bilateral merchandise trade balances with the members of APEC. As can be seen, the largest deficits are with Japan, China, Canada, and Mexico, all important APEC members. Out of a total U.S. merchandise trade deficit of $411.4 billion in 2001, $276.0 billion, or roughly two-thirds of the total deficit, was attributed to just seven APEC partner nations – five in Asia (China, Japan, Taiwan, Malaysia, and South Korea) plus two in North America (Canada and Mexico). reached $306.4 billion in 2000. To the extent that the bilateral trade deficits with APEC countries are being exacerbated by trade barriers that are hindering access to their markets, trade liberalization under APEC may work to increase U.S. exports to those economies and reduce certain bilateral trade deficits. A lessening of a bilateral trade deficit through greater access to foreign markets, however, would tend to change the composition and distribution of the deficit and not necessarily reduce the overall U.S. trade deficit by a corresponding amount.

APEC also raises some fundamental questions for U.S. policy. One is whether a U.S. consensus can be achieved on the APEC vision of free trade and investment in the Asia Pacific region or whether future trade liberalization will be confined primarily to bilateral free-trade arrangements and multilateral trade negotiations under the WTO. Another question is whether the U.S. business community will continue to back the APEC process or whether they view the APEC goals of free trade and investment in the region as too long-term and too lofty to be actually achieved. A further question is whether trade promotion (fast-track) authority should be provided to the President that would cover negotiations under APEC. A final question is whether APEC is worth the effort and resources being devoted to it and whether the United States should continue to participate in it. These questions await a comprehensive domestic policy debate over APEC that is yet to occur.

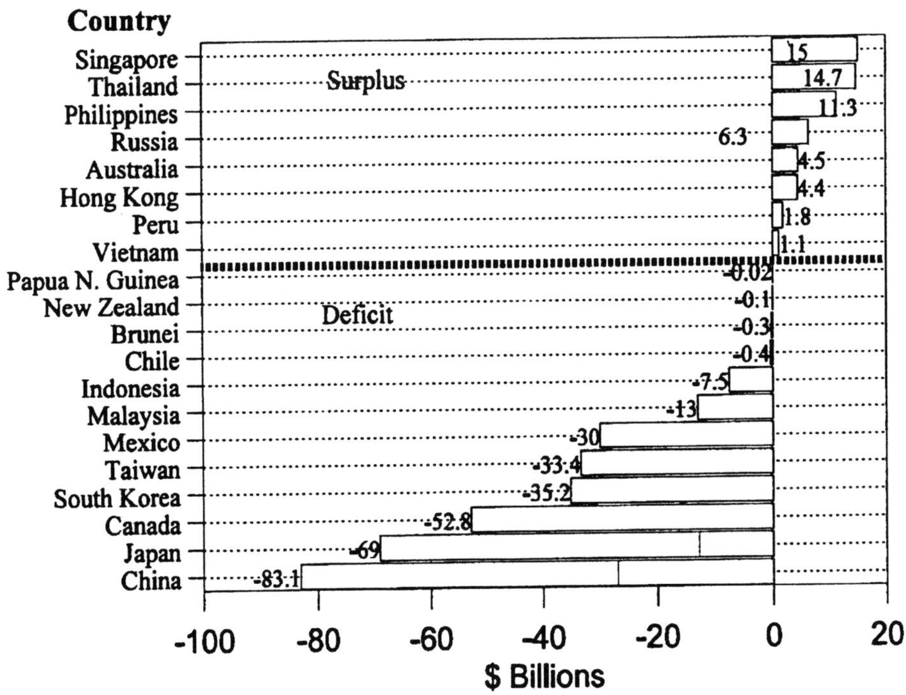

Figure 1. U.S. Merchandise Trade Balances with APEC Members 2001 ($Billion)

Chapter 10

ASIA PACIFIC ECONOMIC COOPERATION (APEC), FREE TRADE, AND THE 2003 SUMMIT IN BANGKOK, THAILAND*

Dick K. Nanto

INTRODUCTION

The Asia Pacific Economic Cooperation (APEC) forum is an association of 21 economies bordering the Pacific Ocean who are working cooperatively to reduce barriers to trade and investment, facilitate the exchange of goods, services, resources, and technical know-how, and strengthen economic and technical cooperation. In 2000, APEC's 21 member economies had a combined Gross Domestic Product of over $19 trillion totaling about 47% of world trade. The members of APEC have declared their intention to establish free trade and investment in the region by the year 2010 for industrialized members and 2020 for the others. For the United States, APEC has become a key institution for pursuing trade and investment liberalization and facilitation in the Asia-Pacific region.

On October 20-21, 2003, the Eleventh APEC Leader's Meeting (informal summit) is to be held in Bangkok, Thailand. It is to be preceded by meetings of ministers, of senior officials from member countries, a CEO summit of business leaders, and the APEC Business Advisory Council meeting. The APEC summit is

* Excerpted from CRS Report RL31038 Updated August 1, 2003.

usually attended by the President, Secretary of State, U.S. Trade Representative, and sometimes the Secretary of Commerce. The theme for APEC 2003 is "A World of Differences: Partnership for the Future" which is intended to bring together the best potential of all APEC economies to confront the challenges of the future, particularly in achieving the APEC goal of free and open trade and investment for developed APEC economies. This central theme is amplified by a series of five sub-themes that are designed to guide APEC's Working Groups and Forums in achieving their goals.

On October 26-27, 2002, the Tenth APEC Leaders' Meeting in Las Cabos, Mexico and other APEC meetings were hosted by Mexico. The theme for APEC 2002 was to expand the benefits of cooperation for economic growth and development and enable the APEC vision to be implemented. The meetings, however, tended to focus on terrorism following attacks in Indonesia, Russia, and the Philippines. President Bush pursued two policy themes: the pending U.N. vote on Iraqi disarmament and the North Korean nuclear program. The leaders declared support for the multilateral trade negotiations under the World Trade Organization (to include the abolition of agricultural export subsidies) and their conclusion by January 1, 2005, agreed to reduce transaction costs in international trade by 5% by 2006, adopted a set of transparency standards, condemned recent terrorist attacks, adopted the Los Cabos Statement on Fighting Terrorism and Promoting Growth, and agreed to toughen security for air and water transport, halt terrorist financing, and increase vigilance in customs, telecommunications, and energy. They also pledged to implement policies on trade and the digital economy.

Prior to the 2002 APEC summit, President Bush met bilaterally with Chinese President Jiang Zemin and Mexican President Vicente Fox and trilaterally with Japanese Prime Minister Junichiro Koizumi and Korean President Kim Dae-Jung. Russian President Vladimir Putin was unable to attend because of the Moscow theater hostage standoff. The meeting with Jiang underscored the importance of China in reining in North Korea's nuclear program. Despite pressure from the United States, Mexican President Fox would not commit to siding with Bush for the United Nations vote on an invasion of Iraq. In a trilateral meeting, the United States, Japan, and South Korea agreed that APEC would declare that North Korea should honor its commitment to give up its nuclear weapons program. Japan stressed that Japan-North Korean normalization talks would not be concluded without full compliance with regard to security issues, including the nuclear issue, and abduction issues.[1]

---

[1] Embassy of Japan. APEC Leaders Called Upon North Korea to Renounce Nuclear Weapons Program. *EOJ Newsletter*, October 28, 2002.

In conjunction with the Mexico APEC summit, the United States announced the Enterprise for ASEAN Initiative, a new trade initiative with the Association of Southeast Asian Nations. This offers the prospect of bilateral free trade agreements between the United States and ASEAN countries that are committed to economic reforms and openness.[2]

In September 2002, APEC Finance ministers agreed to adopt an action plan aimed at boosting efforts to block terrorist financing. The plan would increase the effectiveness of a freeze on terrorist-related assets by fully implementing current laws and working together in the arenas of law enforcement and information sharing.[3]

As in past Leader's meetings, Taiwan's President was not allowed to attend because of objections by China. Taiwan was represented by Nobel prize laureate Lee Yuan-tseh.

APEC has become the primary regional institution in the Asia-Pacific for promoting open trade and practical economic cooperation. It is of interest to Congress because:

- it is becoming a vehicle for pursuing free trade and other initiatives;
- the APEC Leaders' Meeting provides an opportunity for the U.S. President to raise and discuss issues with the heads of other APEC countries;
- concrete trade or investment measures developed under APEC may require a change in existing U.S. laws and legislative approval under the trade promotion authority expedited procedures;
- the U.S. economy is linked to the economies of the Pacific rim through trade, financial investment, and direct investment in subsidiaries in the region; and
- in view of the debate over the effects of NAFTA, the proposed creation of an APEC free-trade arrangement that includes the United States, China, Japan, South Korea, Taiwan, Indonesia, Peru, Russia, Vietnam, Canada, Mexico, and other Asian-Pacific nations could be quite controversial.

The goal of establishing free trade and investment among APEC nations is

[2] White House. Fact Sheet: Enterprise for ASEAN Initiative. October 26, 2002.

[3] Kosukegawa, Yoichi. APEC Agrees to Adopt Action Plan on Terrorist Financing. Japan Economic Newswire. September 5, 2002.

being pursued along three tracks. The first is through liberalizing trade in certain sectors such as information technology. These have been referred to the World Trade Organization in order to bring European and other nations into the agreements and are categorized at the World Trade Organization (WTO) as early voluntary sectoral liberalization (EVSL). The second is through bilateral and regional free trade agreements or by encouraging multilateral trade negotiations under the WTO. The third is through incremental liberalization measures (individual action plans and other programs) undertaken by APEC members.

In the 108th Congress, APEC-related legislation includes the implementation legislation for the U.S.-Singapore (H.R. 2739/S. 1417) and U.S.-Chile (H.R. 2738/S. 1416) free trade agreements (FTAs), which, if passed, will bring to four (including Canada and Mexico) the number of FTAs the United States has concluded with APEC nations. H.Con.Res. 98 would express the sense of the Congress relating to a FTA with Taiwan. U.S. financial support for APEC falls under the State Department's budget under Contributions to International Organizations and has been running at $601,000 per fiscal year.

Debate over trade liberalization under APEC also is likely to address whether provisions dealing with labor and the environment should be included and whether the United States would be able to respond to foreign country violations of labor or environmental standards with economic sanctions or monetary fines (as stipulated in the U.S.-Singapore/Chile FTAs). U.S. participation in APEC also touches on the broader U.S. debate over whether the United States should continue to pursue the expansion of international trade and investment with other nations — particularly through free trade agreements, the effect of trade and globalization on import-sensitive industries, and whether increased trade threatens or enhances U.S. prosperity, employment opportunities, and economic security.

The Administration has been approached by leaders from many other nations who desire to pursue free trade agreements with the United States. In addition to the FTAs with Singapore and Chile, negotiations are underway for FTAs with Morocco, Australia, five Central American nations, the five member nations of the Southern Africa Customs Union, as well as the long-running negotiations to establish a Free Trade Area of the Americas.

The proliferation of regional and bilateral free-trade arrangements in various parts of the world also has generated proposals for other bilateral arrangements among APEC countries.[4] Free trade or preferential trade agreements have been announced or are under discussion among APEC members such as between

[4] Currently, over 130 regional trade agreements are in force. Most provide for reduced trade barriers rather than free trade. Since 1995, the WTO received notifications of 90 agreements.

Singapore and New Zealand, Australia, Japan, Mexico, Canada, and Chile and between Japan and South Korea. The ten countries of the Association of Southeast Asian Nations (ASEAN), Japan, China, and South Korea are considering an Asian free trade bloc (ASEAN + 3). Since 1992, the Association of Southeast Asian Nations (ASEAN) has been phasing in a Free Trade Area (AFTA) for its members, although AFTA's goal is currently to lower tariffs overall and eliminate them only on certain items imported from other member countries.

APEC Institutional Development

APEC began in 1989 as an Australian initiative in recognition of the growing interdependence among Asia-Pacific economies and in response to the free-trade areas which had developed in Europe and North America. Originally intended to exclude the United States and Canada, APEC was to provide an institution and forum for consultation and coordination on economic issues of importance to East Asia and Australia/New Zealand. Ultimately, membership was opened to countries in the Americas.

Membership in APEC initially included twelve economies (Hong Kong and Taiwan are not considered to be countries) but grew to twenty-one. The founding members were the United States, Canada, Japan, South Korea, ASEAN (Brunei, Indonesia, Malaysia, Philippines, Singapore, and Thailand, but not Vietnam), Australia, and New Zealand. In 1991, the People's Republic of China, Taiwan, and Hong Kong joined. In 1993, Mexico and Papua New Guinea were admitted, as was Chile in 1994. In 1997, APEC extended membership to Peru, Russia, and Vietnam (who became members in 1998) and declared a ten-year period of consolidation before additional membership applications would be considered.

The objectives of APEC are:

- to sustain growth and development of the region;
- to encourage the flow of goods, services, capital, and technology;
- to develop and strengthen the multilateral trading system; and ! to reduce barriers to trade in goods and services and investment.

APEC's principles of operation are:

- that APEC is a voluntary association in which participants do not cede powers of regulation or enforcement to a supra-national institution;

- that decisions are based on consensus; and
- that decisions are implemented by individual members on a voluntary basis and by collective actions (the voluntary actions are coordinated and aimed at accomplishing a common goal).

At the 1994 summit in Bogor, Indonesia, APEC leaders signed a declaration setting the goal of free and open trade and investment in APEC. The industrialized economies (United States, Japan, Canada, Australia, New Zealand, Singapore, and possibly others) are to achieve the goal by the year 2010 and the remaining economies to do so by 2020. The United States argued against allowing the additional 10 years for developing economies, but this provision was retained primarily at the insistence of China, South Korea, and Malaysia. The Bogor Declaration is a consensus, not a legal, document.

THE APEC STRUCTURE AND ACTIVITIES

The APEC chair rotates annually and since 1989 has been held by Australia, Singapore, South Korea, Thailand, United States, Indonesia, Japan, the Philippines, Canada, Malaysia, New Zealand, Brunei, China, Mexico, Thailand (in 2003), and Chile (in 2004).

The focal point of APEC activities is the annual **Leaders Meeting** in which the APEC leaders set goals, publicize them, and provide momentum for the process.[5] This is usually held in October or November of each year, and is attended by heads of state except for those from Taiwan (Chinese Taipei) and Hong Kong who, because of China's objections, send other representatives. The major APEC decisions are affirmed and announced at this meeting. This summit meeting also provides a platform for and gives momentum to major APEC initiatives. The Leaders' meeting was begun in 1993 by former President Clinton who invited the leaders to Blake Island near Seattle. Although APEC confines its agenda primarily to economic issues, the heads of state at bilateral meetings conducted before and after the Leader's Meetings have discussed concerns over international security, human rights, and other issues.

Most of the decisions of APEC are first considered in **ministerial meetings**. These include the respective ministers dealing with trade, finance, transportation,

---

[5] Bergsten, C. Fred, ed. *Whither APEC?* Washington, Institute for International Economics, 1997. pp. 3-4. Note: The Leaders Meetings are technically not summits because of Hong Kong and Taiwan whose leaders are not officially heads of state.

telecommunications, human resources development (education), energy, environment, science and technology, and small and medium-sized enterprises. The largest ministerial is the annual **Joint Ministerial Meeting** which precedes the Leaders Meeting. It usually is attended by foreign and trade or commerce ministers from member states. Management of substance is handled under ministerial direction through **Senior Officials Meetings** (held four times per year). In 1993, APEC created a **Secretariat** in Singapore with an Executive Director, 23 officials seconded by member economies for fixed terms and a similar number of locally recruited support staff.

Most of the specific tasks before APEC are being addressed in **committees or working groups** or expert groups that deal with economic issues of importance to the region. For implementing the Bogor declaration, the Committee on Trade and Investment plays the key role. Other committees are the Economic Committee and the Budget and Administrative Committee. APEC also has ten working groups which work on specific areas of cooperation and facilitation: (1) Trade and Investment Data, (2) Trade Promotion, (3) Industrial Science and Technology, (4) Human Resources Development, (5) Energy Cooperation, (6) Marine Resource Conservation, (7) Telecommunications, (8) Transportation, (9) Tourism, and (10) Fisheries. Each working group has one or more shepherds (members) who take responsibility for coordinating the work of the group.

In 1992, APEC formed the **Eminent Persons Group** (EPG) and charged it with developing a "vision" for APEC's future. In 1994, the EPG recommended that APEC establish the goal of free trade, and, in 1995, as it completed its work, it recommended ways to achieve that vision.

In 1995, APEC established the **APEC Business Advisory Council** (ABAC) which consists of up to three members appointed by each APEC member. It provides advice on implementing the APEC agenda and other specific business-related issues.[6]

In 1995, the issue was raised of whether APEC should be expanded to include consideration of regional security issues. Until then, consideration of non-economic issues was confined to bilateral summit meetings surrounding the Leaders Meetings. APEC had carefully kept its distance from security matters for fear that such issues would cause divisions within the group — particularly among China, Taiwan, the United States, Japan, and Russia. Such divisions could thwart cooperation in achieving economic goals. The consensus in 1995 among APEC members seemed to be that regional security issues should be discussed in

[6] U.S. representatives to ABAC are: Gary Benanav, Chairman and CEO of New York Life International; Michael Ducker, Executive Vice President, International, of FedEx, and Robert Prieto, Chairman of Parsons Brinckerhoff.

the ASEAN Regional Forum and other fora rather than in APEC.[7] The ASEAN Regional Forum usually meets after the ASEAN Ministerial Conference and, in addition to the seven members of ASEAN, includes the United States, China, Russia, Japan, South Korea, Australia, New Zealand, Canada, and the European Union. It provides the largest pan-Pacific forum for discussing security issues. In 2001 and 2002, however, terrorism was added to the official agenda of the Leader's Meeting.

THE 1994 BOGOR DECLARATION

In 1994, APEC Leaders announced their commitment to the "Bogor vision" to establish free and open trade and investment in the region by 2010 for industrialized economies and 2020 for developing economies.

THE 1995 OSAKA ACTION AGENDA

Before 1995, APEC declarations and other documents were general statements without specifics on measures to be taken. In 1995 at the meetings in Osaka, Japan, APEC members agreed to an Action Agenda that was intended to translate into reality the aims of APEC) particularly the 1994 Bogor Declaration of achieving free trade and investment among its member economies by the year 2010 or 2020.[8]

The Osaka Action Agenda is the template adopted for APEC work to accomplish its three goals of: (1) trade and investment liberalization, (2) trade and investment facilitation, and (3) economic and technical cooperation. The Agenda laid out nine general principles for members to follow in devising a road map to reach APEC's free-trade goal. These general principles have been used to guide individual APEC members in devising national Action Plans for submission at subsequent meetings.

The **general principles** in the Action Plan included (1) comprehensiveness [all impediments are to be included], (2) WTO-consistency [consistent with World Trade Organization rules], (3) comparability [comparable actions with consideration for different starting points], (4) non-discrimination [benefits to be accorded to all APEC members and also to non-APEC countries], (5)

---

[7] Moosa, Eugene. *Regional Security Remains a Taboo at APEC*. Reuters Newswire Service. November 19, 1995.

[8] Asia Pacific Economic Cooperation. *The Osaka Action Agenda*. November 19, 1995.

transparency [in domestic trade laws and regulations], (6) standstill [no increased protection], (7) simultaneous startcontinuous process-differentiated time tables [all start together in a continuous process to achieve long-term goal], (8) flexibility [in dealing with issues arising from liberalization) a controversial principle that some argue allows for import-sensitive sectors to be liberalized more slowly], and (9) cooperation [to pursue economic and technical cooperation].

The Agenda also outlined actions that APEC economies were to take in fifteen specific areas. These included both actions by individual members and collectively by APEC in tariffs, non-tariff measures, services, investment, standards, customs procedures, intellectual property rights, competition policy, and dispute mediation.

At the 1995 APEC meetings in Osaka, however, Japan led a group (including South Korea, China, and Taiwan) of members who argued for a weak definition of comprehensiveness[9] and insisted on including a general **principle of flexibility** that might allow the country to placate certain import-sensitive sectors (particularly agriculture) by putting them on a slower timetable or possibly even excluding them from complete liberalization. The United States and twelve APEC members viewed the principle of comprehensiveness (coverage of all sectors) as vital to achieving the Bogor vision of free trade in APEC. In Osaka, APEC members reached a compromise that allowed the comprehensiveness principle to remain unchanged but added the principle of flexibility.[10]

At Osaka, Malaysia also argued for making all APEC commitments "voluntary" (meaning that the free-trade target dates would not be binding). For the Bogor Declaration in 1994, Malaysia had attached its objections to establishing the goal of free trade and investment by the year 2010 or 2020. As a compromise, the word "voluntary" was added. The Osaka Leaders' Declaration stated APEC's resolve to "encourage...the evolving efforts of **voluntary liberalization** in the region," but the Osaka Action Agenda clearly declared under the comprehensiveness principle that "the APEC liberalization and facilitation process will be comprehensive, addressing all impediments to achieving the long-

---

[9] October 25, 1995, Representatives Doug Bereuter and Howard L. Berman along with 27 other Members of the U.S. House of Representatives sent a letter to Secretary of State Warren Christopher and USTR Mickey Kantor urging the Clinton Administration not to weaken its resolve to press for "the promised comprehensive and detailed agenda for implementing the Bogor Declaration."

[10] The flexibility principle reads: Considering the different levels of economic development among the APEC economies and the diverse circumstances in each economy, flexibility will be available in dealing with issues arising from such circumstances in the liberalization and facilitation process.

term goal of free and open trade and investment."[11]

APEC members also disagreed over the **non-discrimination principle** or what has been termed "open regionalism." Japan has pressed for the benefits of APEC trade liberalization to be accorded even non-APEC trading partners on a most-favored-nation basis. Japan's government had stated that it thought APEC should not be a trading bloc that discriminates against outsiders. The problem with such unilateral trade liberalization, however, is that it invites free riders and makes generating public support difficult. The United States favored benefits to be accorded non-APEC countries on a reciprocal basis which has been the basis for other negotiations.[12]

The 1996 Manila Action Plan

For the APEC Leaders' Meeting in the Philippines in November 1996, the theme was "from vision to action" meaning that APEC members were taking measures to realize the goal of free and open trade and investment in the region. The APEC economies submitted their first "Individual Action Plans" indicating how they intended to move toward fulfillment of the Bogor goals. Moreover, APEC Leaders called for conclusion of the Information Technology Agreement in the WTO, which acted as a decisive catalyst toward successful completion of this agreement in 1997.

The APEC leaders launched the implementation phase of the free and open trade and investment agenda, delivered business facilitation measures, agreed to advance common goals in the World Trade Organization, developed ways to strengthen economic and technical cooperation, and engaged the business sector as a full partner in the APEC process.[13]

APEC took each of the Individual Action Plans (IAP) by member economies and categorized them according to the fifteen issue areas set forth in the Osaka Action Plan. Although the APEC process relies on concerted unilateral liberalization and does not formally evaluate each IAP, there was considerable pressure placed on countries whose plans fell short. One of the principles of the process is comparability — which means no free riding.

---

[11] APEC. *Osaka Action Agenda*, p. 1.

[12] Johnstone, Christopher B. *An Awkward Dance: The Osaka Summit, Japanese Leadership and the Future of APEC*. JEI Report, October 20, 1995. p. 12.

[13] APEC. *APEC Economic Leaders' Declaration: From Vision to Action*. November 25, 1996.

The 1997 Vancouver Meetings — The Manila Framework

At the time of 1997 Ministerial and Leaders Meetings in Vancouver, British Columbia, several of the Asian APEC members were coping with severe financial crises in which the value of their currencies had plummeted, the value of stocks on their equity markets had dropped, and many of their financial institutions had become insolvent.[14] The International Monetary Fund had already arranged support packages for Thailand and Indonesia and was in the process of doing the same for South Korea.

While the APEC professionals considered the Asian financial crisis a diversion from the APEC agenda for trade and investment liberalization, it added a dimension to a Leaders Meeting that would otherwise have been a rather humdrum event. Prior to the summit, the APEC finance ministers had met in Manila and developed a framework to deal with currency and other financial crises. The ministers rejected a Japanese-backed proposal to establish a separate Asian fund to provide financial support for countries coping with financial difficulties. The Manila Framework was endorsed by the APEC leaders.

The Manila framework included three elements. The first was a strong domestic response by each country involved to create an economic environment that can attract capital and maintain confidence) including to strengthen its banking system. The second was a stronger response by the IMF that included adequate financial support up front to ease any liquidity crisis and to provide the confidence necessary to avoid instability. The third was a cooperative financing mechanism through which the countries of the region would, on a case-by-case basis, backstop IMF financial measures to ensure that adequate resources were available.[15]

At the APEC summit, the leaders also designated fifteen major sectors where the principal goal would be to achieve free trade (tariff elimination) within a short span of years but not later than the year 2005. This represented a restricted, but nevertheless significant, advance on the Bogor Declaration. Detailed market-opening plans were to be concluded by the first half of 1998 with the aim of beginning implementation in 1999. These Early Voluntary Sectoral Liberalization (EVSL) agreements would be patterned after the Information Technology Agreement endorsed in 1996 at the Manila summit and later adopted by the WTO.

---

[14] See CRS Report RL30272, *Global Financial Turmoil, the IMF, and the New Financial Architecture*, by Dick K. Nanto.

[15] Summers, Larry. Press Briefing, Vancouver, BC. November 24, 1997.

Of the fifteen sectors, nine were chosen for action. Of these nine, six had been nominated by the United States. The nine sectors were: environmental goods and services, energy sector, fish and fish products, toys, forest products, gems and jewelry, medical equipment and instruments, chemicals, and a telecommunications mutual recognition arrangement.[16]

Although these EVSL initiatives were begun by APEC, APEC members agreed to send them to the WTO in order to seek participation by the EU and other nations and to make the commitments binding. At the WTO, except for the telecommunications mutual recognition arrangement, the liberalization of these sectors has became entangled in the proposal for a new round of trade negotiations, and progress has stalled.

Another area of focus for the 1997 APEC meetings was trade facilitation and other measures to lower the costs of doing business in the region. The ministers welcomed the achievements under what are called Collective Action Plans that lower costs and reduce barriers to the movement of goods and services, capital, and business people. They endorsed work in these areas, which included: development of the Blueprint for Customs Modernization; establishment of APEC Internet sites; progress on alignment with international standards; increased transparency for acquiring and using intellectual property rights; development of options to enhance the environment for investment; development of model mutual recognition agreements; principles to guide work on dispute mediation; improved mobility for business people (including the APEC Business Travel Card); providing Internet access to member country tariff rates; and development of guidelines for improving the tendering, approval, and regulatory processes for independent power producers.[17]

The 1998 Malaysia Meetings — Sectoral Liberalization

At the 1998 APEC Joint Ministerial and Leader's Meetings held in Kuala Lumpur, Malaysia, President Clinton did not attend because of the imminent bombing of Iraq. The economic turmoil that began in Asia in 1997 was still raging, and APEC Leaders declared that they needed to deal urgently with the financial crisis and committed themselves to pursuing a cooperative growth

---

[16] APEC. *APEC Ministers on Early Sectoral Liberalization* (Annex to APEC Ministers Joint Statement).

[17] APEC. *Asia-Pacific Economic Cooperation (APEC) Ninth Ministerial Meeting Joint Statement.* Available on the World Wide Web at [http://www.apecsec.org.sg].

strategy.

Prior to the APEC meetings, Japan had been urged by the United States and other industrialized nations to stimulate its economy in order to restore domestic demand-led growth, clean up its banking system, further open its markets, deregulate its economy, and do more to help its neighboring countries in crisis. In the weeks leading up to the APEC Leaders' Meeting, Japan did take three measures aimed at restoring its moribund economy and promoting growth in east Asian countries. It announced a stimulus package (its eighth in the 1990s) of public spending and tax cuts worth about $196 billion,[18] unveiled what it called the Miyazawa Initiative — a package of support measures by the Japanese government totaling $30 billion to assist economic recovery in Asian countries,[19] and, jointly with the United States, announced a new $10 billion multilateral initiative aimed at revitalizing private sector growth in Asia.[20]

Another issue had high visibility at the meetings in Malaysia. Malaysian Prime Minister Mahathir Mohamad, who hosted the APEC meetings, had been a severe critic of the APEC trade liberalization process. As the Asian financial crisis battered the Malaysian economy, Mahathir imposed currency controls and restrictions on capital flows to and from Malaysia and stifled dissent within the country.[21] The capital restrictions were in conflict with the goal of free trade and investment in APEC but had attracted sympathy from other nations that had suffered the flight of short-term capital. Mahathir also had his former Deputy Prime Minister Anwar Ibrahim (who had opposed Mahathir and certain of his policies) arrested on a "morals charge." At the APEC summit, no bilateral meetings had been scheduled between President Clinton and Prime Minister Mahathir, and Clinton's non-attendance because of Iraq had an additional muting effect. While in Malaysia for the Joint Ministerial Meeting, Secretary of State Albright met with the wife of the jailed former Deputy Prime Minister, and in a speech at a banquet hosted by Prime Minister Mahathir, Vice President Gore voiced sympathy for Malaysia's pro-democracy forces. Both of these actions

---

[18] Sugawara, Sandra. "Japanese Set Plan for Economy." *Washington Post*, November 16, 1998. P. A21. Japan. Economic Planning Agency. *Outline of Emergency Economic Package*. On Internet at [http://www5.cao.go.jp/98/b/19981116b-taisaku-e.html].

[19] Japan. Ministry of Finance. *New Initiative to Overcome the Asian Currency Crisis*. October 3, 1998. On Internet at [http://www.mof.go.jp/english/if/e1e042.htm].

[20] The White House. Joint Statement by President Clinton and Prime Minister Obuchi. November 16, 1998. On Internet at [http://www.mof.go.jp/english/if/e1e054.htm].

[21] For a summary of the controls, see Aziz, Zeti Akhtar. *Preparing for the New International Financial Architecture: Malaysia's Programme*. Speech at the International Conference on "Managing the Asian Financial Crisis: Lessons & Challenges" on November 2-3, 1998. On Internet at [http://www.bnm.gov.my/spch/1998/1102.htm].

brought strong negative reactions from Malaysian officials.[22]

THE 1999 NEW ZEALAND SUMMIT — END OF FINANCIAL CRISIS

On September 12-13, 1999, the Seventh APEC Leaders Meeting was held in Auckland, New Zealand. The 1999 APEC meetings occurred earlier than their usual time because the World Trade Organization's Ministerial Conference was to be held in Seattle on November 30-December 3, 1999. APEC wanted to complete its recommendations for the WTO with enough time for them to be considered for the WTO Conference. The APEC leaders endorsed the launching of a new WTO round of multilateral trade negotiations and agreed that the new round of trade negotiations should: (1) include industrial tariffs as well as mandated negotiations on services and agriculture, (2) lead to timely and effective improvements in market access to the benefit of all participants, particularly developing countries, (3) have a balanced and sufficiently broad-based agenda, and (4) be concluded within three years as a single package but which would not preclude the possibility of early results on a provisional basis. For the new WTO round, the APEC leaders also: (5) supported the abolition of agricultural export subsidies and unjustifiable export restrictions, (6) agreed that the current moratorium on duties on electronic commerce should be extended, and (7) endorsed efforts to achieve an agreement on transparency in government procurement.[23]

The APEC summit occurred at a time of increasing violence in East Timor following its vote for independence from Indonesia. APEC leaders took advantage of bilateral meetings with each other to put pressure on Indonesia to allow international peacekeepers into the country. While APEC was in session, Indonesian President Habibie bowed to international concerns and agreed to allow a United Nations peacekeeping force into East Timor.[24]

The APEC summit also occurred when the Asian economies appeared to be recovering from the economic crisis that had beset the region and certain other nations of the world since July 1997. As Thailand, Indonesia, the Philippines,

---

[22] Blustein, Paul. "Gore Remarks Anger Malaysian Leaders." *Washington Post*. November 17, 1998. P. A29.

[23] APEC Secretariat. Leaders' Declaration - New Zealand. Press Release 47/99, September 13, 1999. On Internet at [http://www.apecsec.org.sg]. U.S. Trade Representative. Statement of United States Trade Representative Charlene Barshefsky at the Conclusion of the APEC Ministerial Sessions in Auckland, New Zealand. Press Release 99-73, September 10, 1999.

[24] Richburg, Keith B. "Jakarta Asks U.N. Force to End E. Timor Turmoil." *Washington Post*, September 13, 1999. p. 1A.

South Korea, Japan, Hong Kong, and other Asian countries dropped into recession, their enthusiasm for further opening of their markets had waned. However, with the exception of Indonesia, the APEC economies seemed to have turned the corner, and there was heightened recognition that open, transparent, and well-governed markets were key to a return to sustained economic growth and prosperity. The general assessment of APEC's ability to cope with the Asian financial crisis, however, seemed to be that APEC really did little substantive work and that the International Monetary Fund, World Bank, the U.S. Treasury, and other players in international financial markets carried the burden of coping with the crisis.[25] In order to bring APEC finance ministers more into the mainstream of APEC activities, the finance ministerial meeting was moved to the period immediately preceding the Leaders meeting.

THE 2000 BRUNEI SUMMIT — TOWARD BILATERAL FTAS

On November 15-16, 2000, the Eighth APEC Leaders' Meeting was held in Bandar Seri Begawan, Brunei. During the bilateral meeting with Singapore, the United States and Singapore announced that they would begin negotiations on a bilateral free trade agreement.[26] Given the stalled start of the WTO multilateral negotiations, more and more countries were opting to proceed with bilateral free trade agreements. During other bilateral meetings, the United States, New Zealand, Singapore, Brunei, and Chile agreed in principle to an "open skies" pact (eliminating restrictions on airline flights, prices, and routes among themselves),[27] and the U.S. and China announced that China would ban certain missile-related exports in exchange for a lifting of U.S. sanctions prohibiting Chinese launches of American satellites.[28]

In the Brunei summit, the APEC leaders reaffirmed their determination to realize the goal of free and open trade and investment among member economies and agreed on the need to expeditiously launch a new round of trade negotiations under the World Trade Organization in 2001. In a concession to developing country members (particularly Malaysia), the leaders called for a balanced and sufficiently broad-based agenda that would respond to the interests and concerns

---

[25] See, for example, Sanger, David E. "Some Birthday Cake for a Toothless Wonder." *New York Times*, September 12, 1999.

[26] See CRS Report RS20755, *Singapore-U.S. Free Trade Agreement*, by Dick K. Nanto.

[27] U.S. Department of Transportation. United States, Asia-Pacific Aviation Partners Enter Multilateral Open Skies Agreement. DOT Press Release 222-00, November 15, 2000.

[28] Perlez, Jane. China to Stop Selling A-Arms Delivery Systems. *New York Times*, November 21, 2000. P. A12.

of all WTO members to be finalized as soon as possible in 2001. The APEC communique also stated that China should be accepted into the WTO soon, followed by Taiwan and sometime later by Russia and Vietnam; that the people in every economy should have access to information and services offered via the Internet by 2010; and that countries recovering from the 1997-98 Asian financial crisis should keep up with painful economic reforms even though their economies were then recovering.[29]

THE 2001 SHANGHAI SUMMIT — POST 9/11

On October 20-21, 2001, the Ninth APEC Leaders' Meeting (summit) was held in Shanghai, China. For 2001, China hosted the Leaders' Meeting and, in consultation with other APEC members, set the major agenda items. The official theme for 2001 was "Meeting New Challenges in the New Century: Achieving Common Prosperity through Participation and Cooperation" with sub-themes of: (1) sharing the benefits of globalization and the new economy, (2) advancing trade and investment, and (3) promoting sustained economic growth. The war on terrorism and slowing world economic growth, however, dominated discussions. The leaders' statement on counter-terrorism was the first time APEC dealt explicitly with a noneconomic issue. In the statement, the leaders condemned the attacks on the United States, committed themselves to preventing and suppressing all forms of terrorists acts in the future, to enhance counter-terrorism cooperation, and take appropriate financial measures to prevent the flow of funds to terrorists.[30] APEC leaders also reaffirmed the goal of achieving free trade and investment among APEC members and strongly supported the launch of the new round of multilateral trade negotiations under the World Trade Organization.

At the Shanghai meeting, the leaders also issued the Shanghai Accord in which they committed themselves to broaden APEC's vision for the future by identifying a conceptual and policy framework to guide APEC in the new century. The Accord included clarifying APEC's roadmap for achieving the free trade and investment goals on schedule with an assessment of overall progress in 2005, promoting the adoption of appropriate trade policies for the New Economy, following up on the APEC Trade Facilitation Principles, pursuing greater

---

[29] APEC Secretariat. Delivering to the Community, APEC Economic Leaders' Declaration, Bandar Seri Begawan, Brueni Darussalam. November 16, 2000. On Internet at [http://www.apecsec.org.sg].

[30] Asia Pacific Economic Cooperation. APEC Leaders Statement on Counter-terrorism. Shanghai, China, October 21, 2001.

transparency in economic governance, and strengthening APEC's implementation mechanism.[31]

POLICY ASSESSMENT AND IMPLICATIONS

Trade liberalization under APEC is nowhere near as far along as that under either the European Union or the North America Free Trade Agreement. APEC's goal of free trade is to be phased in over the next two decades. Only the framework now exists to lead APEC members toward that goal. APEC is not a negotiating body nor are its decisions legally binding on its members. The APEC process has been called "concerted unilateral action" in which a set of principles and guidelines are agreed to by APEC members and used to steer individual member actions. Rather than a trade bloc, APEC can be characterized as a building block toward greater trade liberalization and cooperation not only within the organization, itself, but in broader contexts, such as in the World Trade Organization. The APEC work programs are conducted on the basis of open dialogue with equal respect for the views of all participants — both the member countries and, to a certain extent, private business interests. This consensus-based decision making, however, tends to be slow and cumbersome.

When APEC began, many thought it would be just another "talk shop." The movement in APEC toward voluntary free trade and investment liberalization, however, has gone beyond initial expectations and seems to reflect a change in world economic circumstances and attitudes. The nations belonging to the WTO already have agreed to reduce tariffs and eliminate most non-tariff barriers. For the industrialized nations, in particular, tariffs already are so low in many sectors that some argue that dropping them entirely would make little difference. Until the onset of the Asian financial crisis in 1997, many nations were discovering the advantages of free trade and unfettered foreign investment in today's fast moving, consumeroriented markets. A perception was developing that closed markets and unfriendly investment climates can cause economies to lose rather than create employment opportunities. Since the 1997-99 Asian financial crisis and ensuing slow-down in economic growth, however, some nations are taking a second look at the costs as well as advantages of free trade and capital flows — particularly short-term capital flows between wealthy and developing economies.

In terms of U.S. interests, APEC promotes trade and cooperation among economies that have been the most dynamic in the world, encourages open trading

[31] APEC. APEC Economic Leaders' Declaration, Shanghai, China. October 21, 2001.

systems rather than trading blocs, helps U.S. businesses remain engaged in the region, and provides the Asia-Pacific region with a counterweight to the European Union. In response to APEC, the European Union in 1996 initiated ASEM, the Asia-Europe Meeting, which excludes the Americas.[32] At the same time, countries in the Americas are pursuing the Free Trade Area of the Americas (FTAA) a free-trade arrangement that would stretch from Canada to Chile.[33]

Critics of APEC include those who (1) assert that liberalized trade and investment has been primarily a one-way street that benefits trading partners more than the United States; (2) are concerned that the U.S. President should not be meeting annually with the heads of state of countries with alleged human rights problems (for example, China, Indonesia, and Vietnam), and (3) place higher priority on environmental considerations than trade.

Some import sensitive sectors also have opposed further opening of U.S. markets and more free trade agreements. They fear that APEC free trade could become a two-edged sword. U.S. firms could gain greater access to Asian and South American markets, but exporters from those regions also would gain more access to U.S. markets. There are concerns that this could hurt previously protected American industries, such as apparel, agriculture, steel, and motor vehicles (notably, pickup trucks). Some in these import-sensitive industries have opposed liberalized imports from Asia and Latin America. Also, in light of the intense opposition from some in the United States concerning granting China the trade privileges of normal-trade-relations (most-favored-nation) status and allowing it to join the World Trade Organization, the question remains of how Americans would respond to establishing free trade with that nation. Furthermore, given the hidden barriers to trade and investment in countries like Japan (close business relationships, interlocking corporate organizations, etc.), some have questioned whether free trade with Japan might be a one-way street. Would Japanese exporters gain unlimited access to the U.S. market, while American exporters still would face a web of private trade barriers in Japan?

APEC is maturing as an organization and has now drawn most major players in the Asia-Pacific region into its membership. Its long-range goals are lofty, but it seems to be moving steadily toward achieving them. It is becoming a credible

---

[32] ASEM met for the first time, on March 1-2, 1996, in Bangkok, Thailand. It included Heads of State and Government of ten Asian Nations (ASEAN plus China, Japan, and Korea) and fourteen members of the European Union plus the European Commission. The initial purpose has been to allow the leaders to become better acquainted with each other in order to build a foundation for further and continued cooperation among the participating countries. For information on U.S.-EU trade, see CRS Report 97-734, *The Transatlantic Business Dialogue*, by Glennon Harrison.

[33] See CRS Report RS20864, *A Free Trade Area of the Americas: Status of Negotiations and Major Policy Issues*, by J. F. Hornbeck.

vehicle to discuss and coordinate issues in the region as well as to achieve trade and investment liberalization. The Asian financial crisis dampened enthusiasm for further opening of markets, but the crisis also underlined the need for market discipline in allocating financial resources. Market discipline occurs partly through liberalized trade and capital flows.

The Individual Action Plans that are to bring the member economies closer to the APEC goal of free trade and investment in the region contain many significant actions. Most tariff reductions, however, reflect what member governments already are committed to do in the World Trade Organization. Some regulations have been changed in response to APEC efforts, but for most countries, only a few actions to reduce tariffs or ease foreign investment requirements have been taken specifically to achieve the APEC goals. The time has arrived, however, when APEC members will have to consider concrete measures that go beyond those already scheduled in order to achieve the goals of the Bogor Declaration.

A strategy that countries are pursuing to go beyond their WTO obligations is to negotiate free-trade agreements with other APEC members. In view of the difficulty in reaching a consensus in the multilateral trade negotiations under the WTO and the slow progress under APEC, many individual members are electing to go down the route of bilateral or regional free trade agreements.

On the other hand, within the United States, those who question the expansion of international trade and investment often argue that the U.S. should not pursue more free-trade arrangements because of human rights, economic, and other concerns. Import-sensitive industries are among those who often oppose granting other nations greater access to U.S. markets. They also are less interested in access to foreign markets that might be accorded through trade and investment liberalization. Controversy also continues over the extent to which environmental and labor issues are handled in such agreements. Anti-globalization protesters who have directed their efforts mainly to oppose WTO, International Monetary Fund, and World Bank activities also could oppose further trade liberalization under APEC.

APEC is also facing the growing pains of any new organization. Some of its committees and working groups have overlapping interests. The number of meetings is increasing, and travel requirements are rising for participants. Still, it has, so far, avoided forming a large bureaucracy such as those in the Organization for Economic Cooperation and Development or the European Union. Also, it has expanded its scope to address financial problems as well as trade and investment.

In August 2002, the APEC International Assessment Network released a report that examined APEC's effectiveness and made recommendations on how it might be improved.[34] The report concluded that: (1) APEC's management structures have grown both too complex and too weak to meet the needs of a growing organization and need a thorough overhaul; (2) APEC's decision making rules, where the requirements of 100% agreement too often produce paralysis, should be made more flexible; (3) APEC's outreach, which in earlier years was a source of strength, has languished, precisely when the private sector, academic experts, and other civil society actors are gaining weight in global diplomacy; (4) APEC's product has become scattered, and APEC needs to clarify its roles in market liberalization, in economic cooperation, and in policy development; and (5) APEC's financial structure is woefully inadequate in comparison to APEC's goals and objectives. The report also recommended several reforms including having the Executive Director serve a multi-year term with new middle managers, hiring more experts, a flexible consensus for decision making, recognizing policy development as one of its core missions, and rationalizing its financial structure.

For the United States, a problem related to APEC is that the U.S. merchandise trade balance with the APEC member economies has been deteriorating. This can be attributed mostly to U.S. macroeconomic conditions, but the political repercussions in the United States from this rising trade deficit could combine with specific trade disputes to have a negative impact on overall trade relations with some of the APEC countries such as China and Japan.

Figure 1 shows U.S. bilateral merchandise trade balances with the members of APEC. As can be seen, the largest deficits are with China, Japan, Canada, and Mexico, all important APEC members. Out of a total U.S. merchandise trade deficit of $468.3 billion in 2002, $299.9 billion, or roughly two-thirds of the total deficit, was attributed to just seven APEC partner nations — five in Asia (China, Japan, Taiwan, Malaysia, and South Korea) plus two in North America (Canada and Mexico). To the extent that the bilateral trade deficits with APEC countries are being exacerbated by trade barriers that are hindering access to their markets, trade liberalization under APEC may work to increase U.S. exports to those economies and reduce certain bilateral trade deficits. A lessening of a bilateral trade deficit through greater access to foreign markets, however, would tend to change the composition and distribution of the deficit and not necessarily reduce the overall U.S. trade deficit by a corresponding amount.

[34] APEC International Assessment Network. *Remaking APEC as an Institution*, The Third APIAN Policy Report, August 2002.

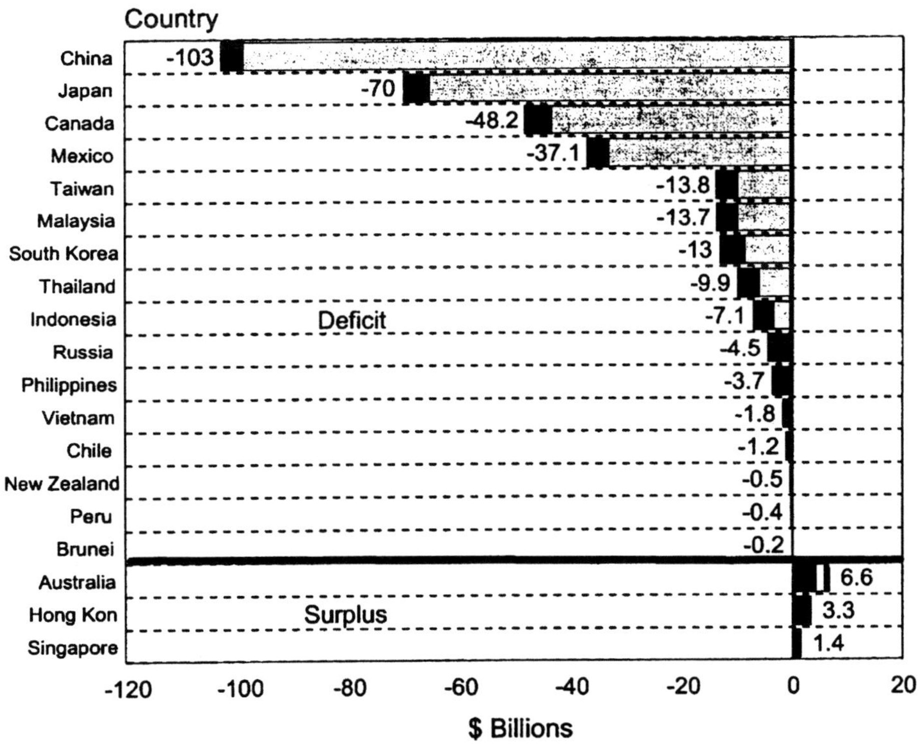

Source: U.S. Department of Commerce (Census Bureau)

Figure 1. U.S. Merchandise Trade Balances with APEC Countries/Economies, 2002

APEC also raises some fundamental questions for U.S. policy. One is whether a U.S. consensus can be achieved on the APEC vision of free trade and investment in the Asia Pacific region or whether future trade liberalization will be confined primarily to bilateral free-trade arrangements and multilateral trade negotiations under the WTO. Another question is whether the U.S. business community will continue to back the APEC process or whether they view the APEC goals of free trade and investment in the region as too long-term and too lofty to be actually achieved. A final question is whether APEC is worth the effort and resources (although small) being devoted to it and whether the United States should continue to participate in it. These questions await a comprehensive domestic policy debate over APEC that is yet to occur.

INDEX

F

G

H

I

V

W

Y